D0806400

day
skipper
2005

Written by Penny Haire
Illustrations by Sarah Selman
Edited by Simon Jinks
Layout by Battcreative
Printed by WorldPrint

www.rya.org.uk

Royal Yachting Association
RYA House, Ensign Way, Hamble, Southampton SO31 4YA
Tel: 0845 345 0400 Fax: 0845 345 0329
email: training@rya.org.uk website: www.rya.org.uk

CONTENTS

The skills required to safely skipper a boat, navigate from port to port and moor up at the end of the day are the same the world over. However, there are two notable differences that can catch-out the unwary sailor when sailing in different parts of the world; the circulation of weather patterns in the Northern and Southern hemispheres and the layout of buoyage in the Eastern and Western Hemispheres. Both of these differences are covered in the book, but ensure you use the correct system for your sailing area.

Charts reproduced throughout this book are for training purposes only. On no account should they be used for navigation.

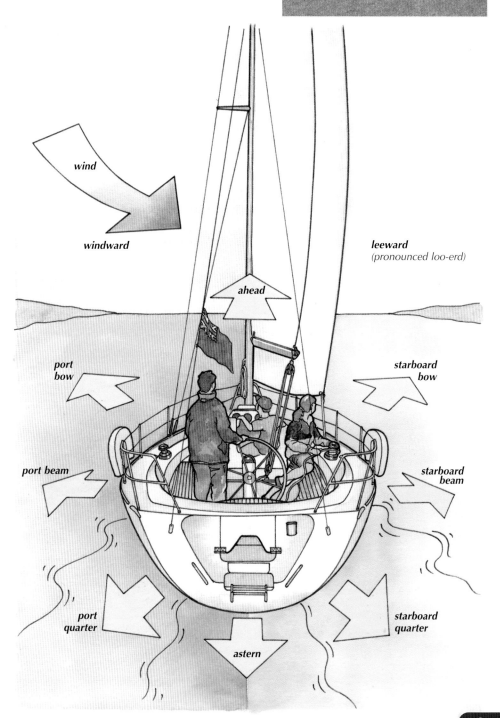

wind

windward

leeward
(pronounced loo-erd)

ahead

port
bow

starboard
bow

port beam

starboard
beam

port
quarter

starboard
quarter

astern

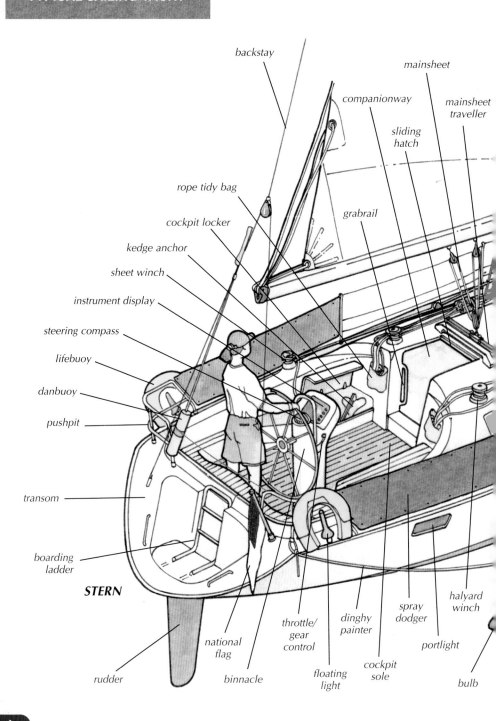

backstay

mainsheet

companionway

mainsheet traveller

sliding hatch

rope tidy bag

grabrail

cockpit locker

kedge anchor

sheet winch

instrument display

steering compass

lifebuoy

danbuoy

pushpit

transom

boarding ladder

STERN

halyard winch

spray dodger

dinghy painter

throttle/ gear control

national flag

portlight

rudder

binnacle

floating light

cockpit sole

bulb

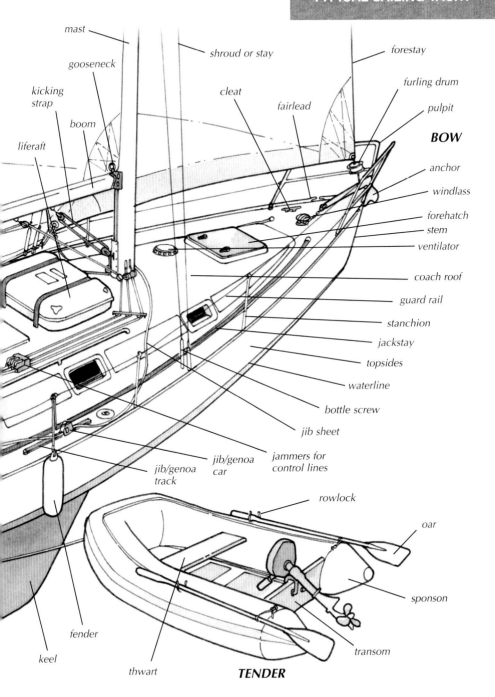

mast

gooseneck

shroud or stay

forestay

kicking
strap

cleat

furling drum

fairlead

pulpit

boom

BOW

liferaft

anchor

windlass

forehatch

stem

ventilator

coach roof

guard rail

stanchion

jackstay

topsides

waterline

bottle screw

jib sheet

jammers for
control lines

jib/genoa
car

jib/genoa
track

rowlock

oar

sponson

fender

transom

keel

thwart

TENDER

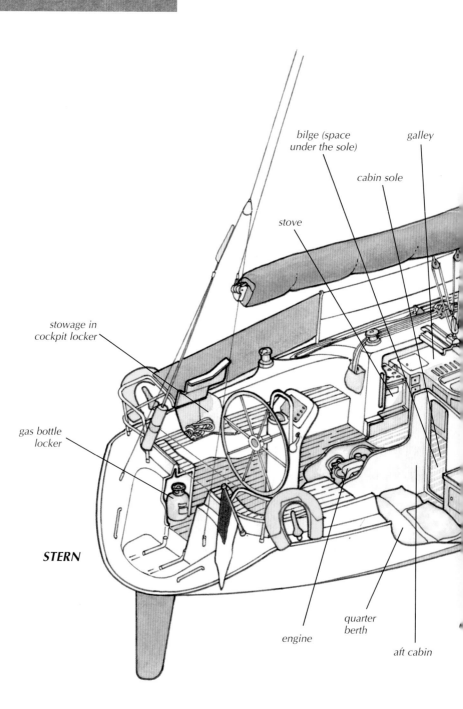

bilge (space under the sole)

galley

cabin sole

stove

stowage in cockpit locker

gas bottle locker

STERN

engine

quarter berth

aft cabin

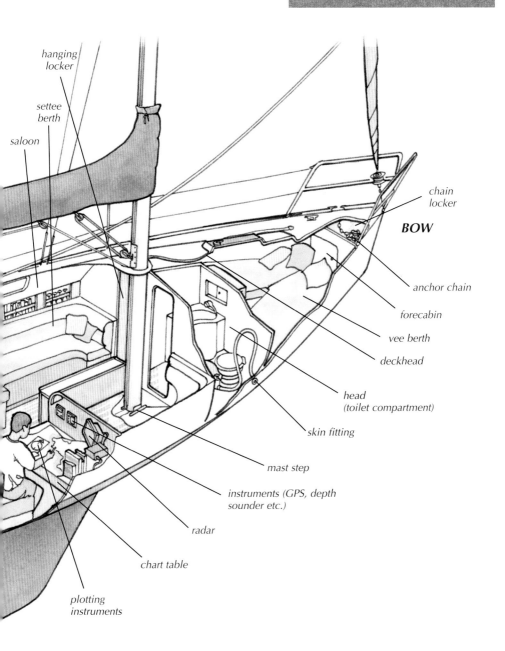

hanging
locker

settee
berth

saloon

chain
locker

BOW

anchor chain

forecabin

vee berth

deckhead

head
(toilet compartment)

skin fitting

mast step

instruments (GPS, depth
sounder etc.)

radar

chart table

plotting
instruments

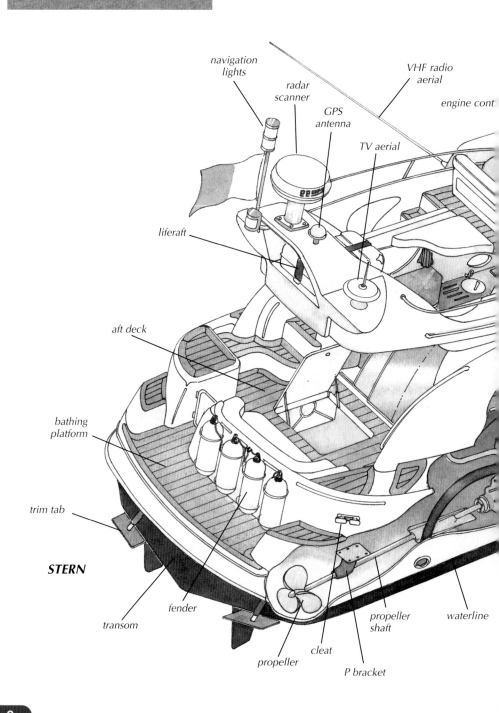

navigation lights

radar scanner

VHF radio aerial

GPS antenna

engine cont

TV aerial

liferaft

aft deck

bathing platform

trim tab

STERN

transom

fender

propeller

cleat

propeller shaft

P bracket

waterline

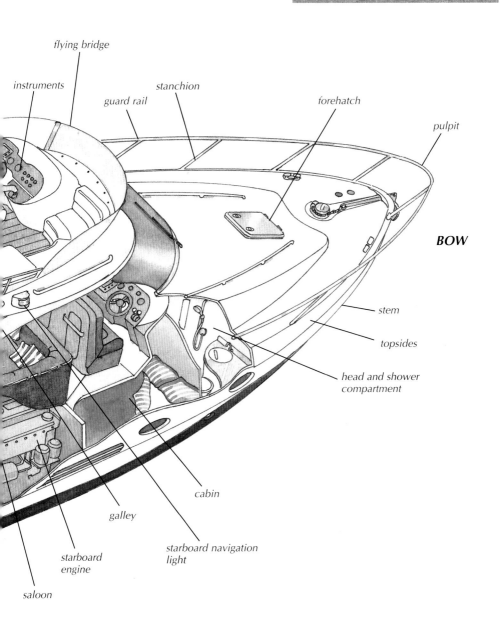

flying bridge

instruments

guard rail

stanchion

forehatch

pulpit

BOW

stem

topsides

head and shower
compartment

cabin

galley

starboard navigation
light

starboard
engine

saloon

You can't sail closer than about 45° to the wind otherwise the sails flap and the boat slows down very quickly.

To make progress to windward (into the wind) you must travel in a series of zigzags, each at 45° to the wind.

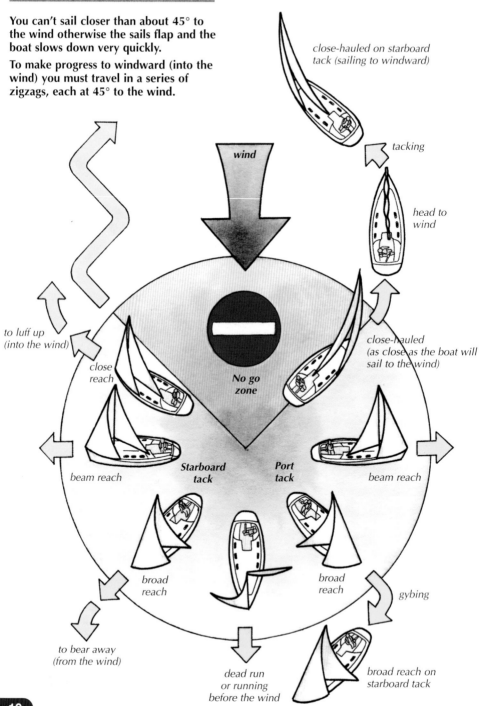

close-hauled on starboard tack (sailing to windward)

tacking

head to wind

to luff up (into the wind)

close-hauled (as close as the boat will sail to the wind)

close reach

No go zone

Starboard tack

Port tack

beam reach

beam reach

broad reach

broad reach

gybing

to bear away (from the wind)

dead run or running before the wind

broad reach on starboard tack

When you put a spoon into running water it is sucked into the flow.

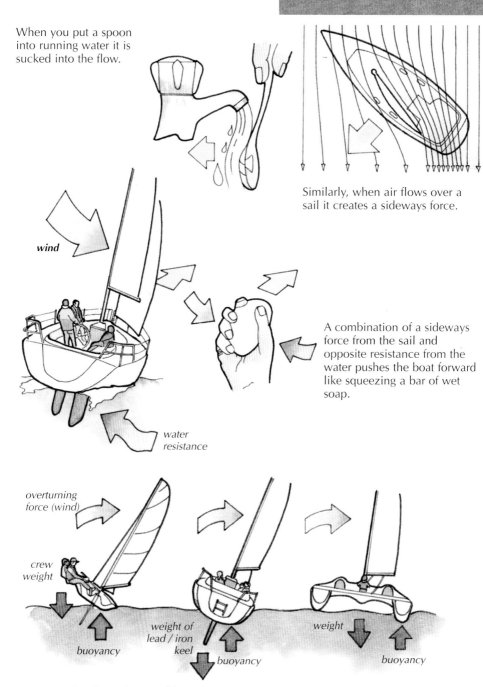

Similarly, when air flows over a sail it creates a sideways force.

wind

A combination of a sideways force from the sail and opposite resistance from the water pushes the boat forward like squeezing a bar of wet soap.

water resistance

overturning force (wind)

crew weight

buoyancy

weight of lead / iron keel

buoyancy

weight

buoyancy

A sailing boat does not blow over as the force of the wind is counterbalanced by weight and buoyancy.

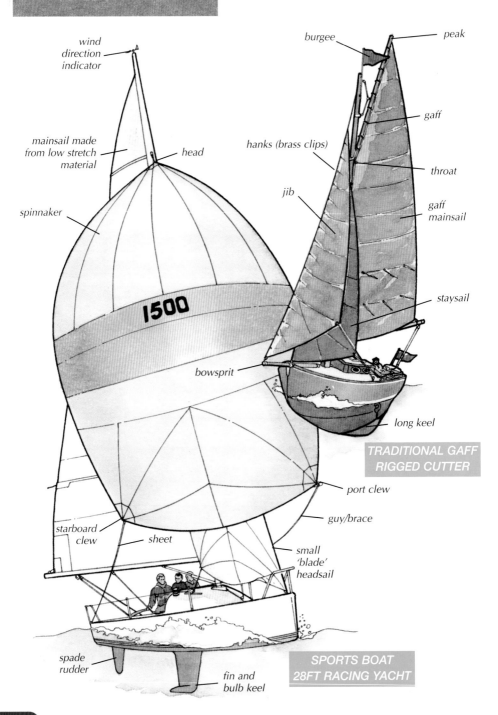

wind direction indicator

burgee

peak

gaff

mainsail made from low stretch material

head

hanks (brass clips)

throat

spinnaker

jib

gaff mainsail

staysail

1500

bowsprit

long keel

TRADITIONAL GAFF RIGGED CUTTER

port clew

guy/brace

starboard clew

sheet

small 'blade' headsail

spade rudder

fin and bulb keel

SPORTS BOAT 28FT RACING YACHT

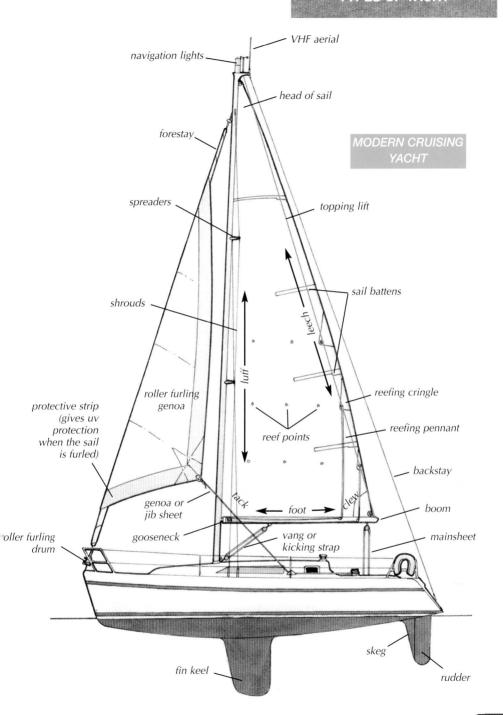

navigation lights

VHF aerial

head of sail

forestay

MODERN CRUISING YACHT

spreaders

topping lift

sail battens

shrouds

leech

luff

reefing cringle

roller furling genoa

reef points

reefing pennant

protective strip (gives uv protection when the sail is furled)

backstay

tack

foot

clew

boom

genoa or jib sheet

gooseneck

vang or kicking strap

mainsheet

roller furling drum

skeg

fin keel

rudder

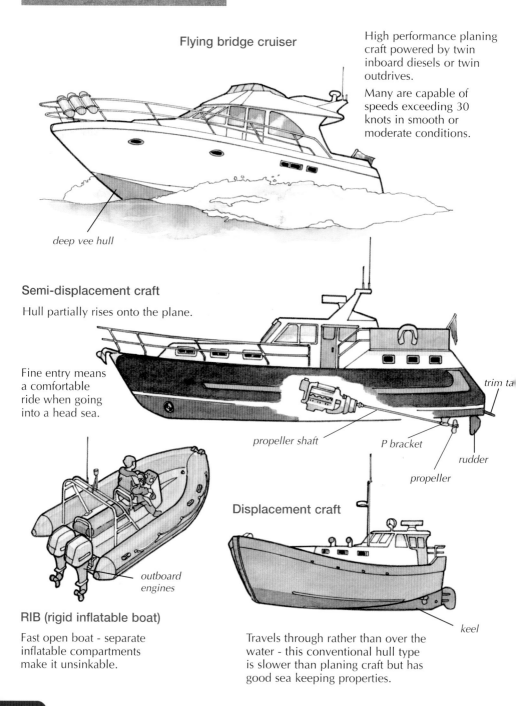

Flying bridge cruiser

High performance planing craft powered by twin inboard diesels or twin outdrives.

Many are capable of speeds exceeding 30 knots in smooth or moderate conditions.

deep vee hull

Semi-displacement craft

Hull partially rises onto the plane.

Fine entry means a comfortable ride when going into a head sea.

trim ta

propeller shaft   *P bracket*

rudder

propeller

Displacement craft

outboard engines

RIB (rigid inflatable boat)

Fast open boat - separate inflatable compartments make it unsinkable.

keel

Travels through rather than over the water - this conventional hull type is slower than planing craft but has good sea keeping properties.

High performance planing craft

Boat rides over the surface of the water.

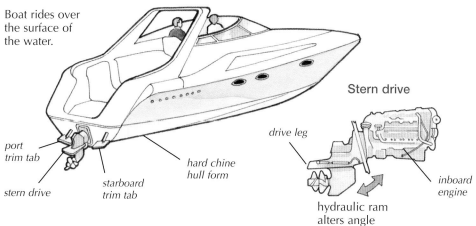

port trim tab

stern drive

starboard trim tab

hard chine hull form

Stern drive

drive leg

hydraulic ram alters angle

inboard engine

TRIM

Changing the trim will affect the way a boat behaves in different conditions. Experiment to find how your boat reacts.

Power trim

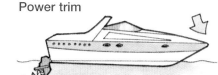

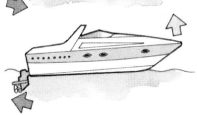

Outdrive leg in - drops the bow for going into a head sea reduces slamming.

Outdrive leg out - lifts the bow in a following sea.

Trim tabs in operation

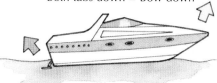

Both tabs down = Bow down

Both tabs up = Bow up

Port tab = Port up

Starboard tab = Starboard up

Round turn and two half hitches

Multipurpose knot. Can be untied under tension.

Rolling hitch

Used when you need a knot that won't slip when pulled at an angle. Ideal for taking the strain off another rope.

Reef knot

Mainly used for tying in reef points. Not very secure.

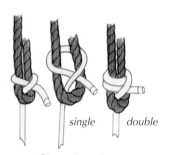

single   *double*

Sheet bend

Used for joining two ropes.

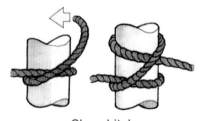

Clove hitch

Quick to tie and easy to adjust. Ideal for securing fenders.

Figure of eight

Easy to tie stopper knot - stops rope escaping.

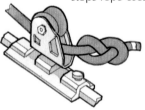

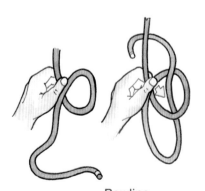

Bowline

Makes a fixed eye in a rope which is very secure but can't be untied under tension. Many uses such as attaching jibsheets to sails and for loops in mooring lines.

Making fast to a cleat

Rope led to 'open' side of cleat.

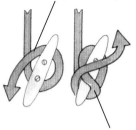

Follow with several figure of eights and one more round turn to increase friction.

Jammer - holds rope securely, like a cleat.

When releasing a rope under load don't hold it close to the jammer - take the strain on a winch.

Winching techniques

Using a winch gives more power for pulling in ropes.

Use the selftailer to grip the rope before you winch

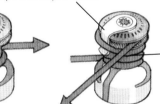

Add more turns for maximum friction.

Always wind the rope clockwise round the drum'.

Turn the handle either way to pull in the rope.

Keep the lead low to avoid a riding turn.

When letting out gently ease rope round drum with palm of hand.

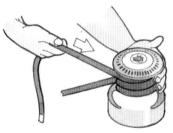

Always have your thumbs uppermost - take care not to trap fingers or thumbs between the rope and the winch.

Letting fly - flip the rope quickly off the drum to release rope when tacking or gybing.

ALONGSIDE A WALL

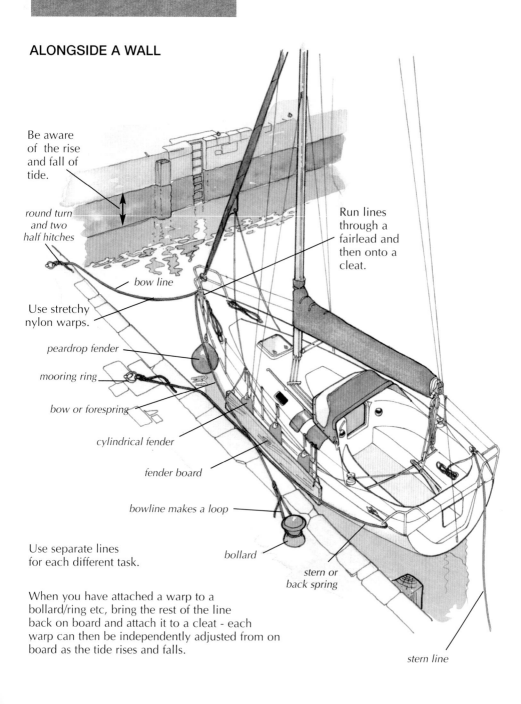

Be aware of the rise and fall of tide.

round turn and two half hitches

Run lines through a fairlead and then onto a cleat.

bow line

Use stretchy nylon warps.

peardrop fender

mooring ring

bow or forespring

cylindrical fender

fender board

bowline makes a loop

Use separate lines for each different task.

bollard

stern or back spring

When you have attached a warp to a bollard/ring etc, bring the rest of the line back on board and attach it to a cleat - each warp can then be independently adjusted from on board as the tide rises and falls.

stern line

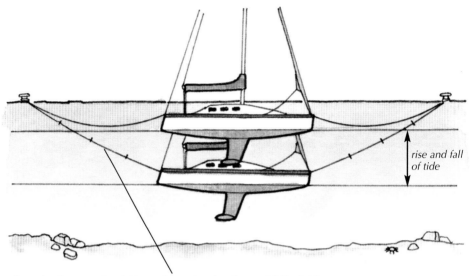

Length of warps should be at least 4 x the rise and fall of tide.

rise and fall of tide

In a raft

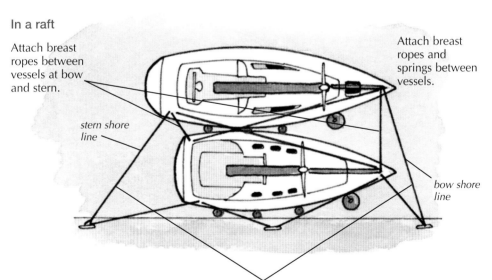

Attach breast ropes between vessels at bow and stern.

Attach breast ropes and springs between vessels.

stern shore line

bow shore line

Outside boat should take bow and stern lines ashore to minimise strain on the inside boat's shore lines.

ON A FLOATING PONTOON

You should not have to
adjust lines as the tide
rises and falls.

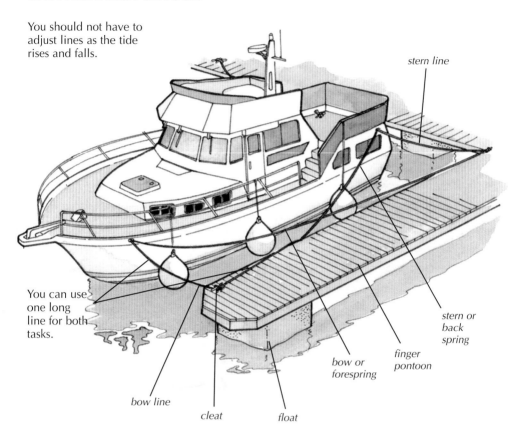

stern line

You can use
one long
line for both
tasks.

*stern or
back
spring*

*finger
pontoon*

*bow or
forespring*

bow line

cleat

float

IN A PEN

Stern lines are attached to piles and the bow lines are attached to a wall or pontoon. Usually the windward lines are attached first.

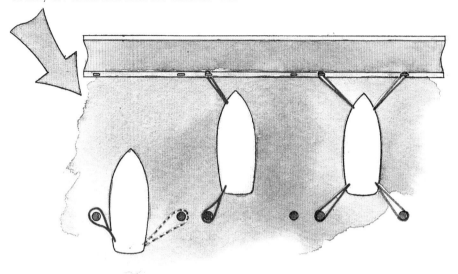

In some countries one of the piles is replaced by a pontoon for ease of access to the shore. The lines are adjusted to allow access from the steps or amidships. Pick-up-lines are usually supplied on the piles to aid retrieval.

bow line

ring rises and falls with tide

pick-up lines

stern line

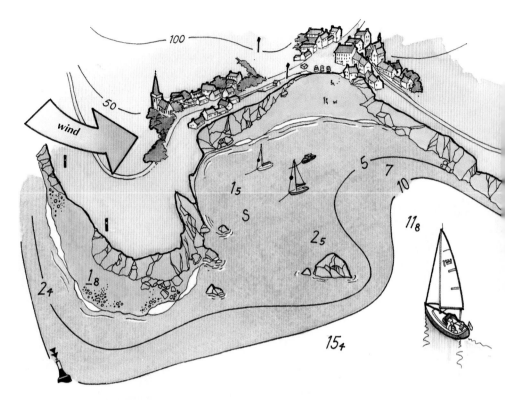

Selecting an anchorage

- Will you be sheltered? - look for maximum protection from wind, swell and tide.

- What is the sea bed like? - look at the chart symbols - mud and sand give better holding than rock or shingle.

- What will the tide do during your stay? - calculate the tide times and heights - make sure that you don't pick a spot where you will ground as the tide falls.

- Will you have enough swinging room? - allow for other boats, isolated rocks etc.

- Prepare the amount of anchor chain or warp that you need before dropping the anchor.

You don't necessarily need to anchor at the position of the anchor symbol. This is just a recommendation.

Avoid anchoring on or near the leading line - other boats may be coming in.

There will be much less tidal flow in the bay than outside.

Scope

The scope of chain or warp you need depends on the maximum depth of water you expect during your stay.

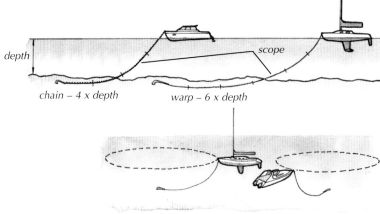

depth

scope

chain – 4 x depth   warp – 6 x depth

Always allow enough swinging room to account for wind and tide. Bear in mind that light/flat-bottomed boats will lie differently to deeper draft/low windage boats.

TYPES OF ANCHOR

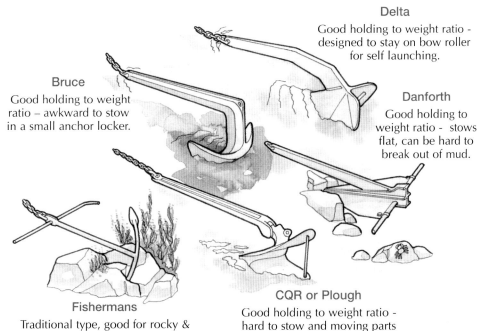

Delta
Good holding to weight ratio - designed to stay on bow roller for self launching.

Bruce
Good holding to weight ratio – awkward to stow in a small anchor locker.

Danforth
Good holding to weight ratio - stows flat, can be hard to break out of mud.

Fishermans
Traditional type, good for rocky & weedy bottoms – awkward to stow and poor holding power in sand and mud.

CQR or Plough
Good holding to weight ratio - hard to stow and moving parts can capsize.

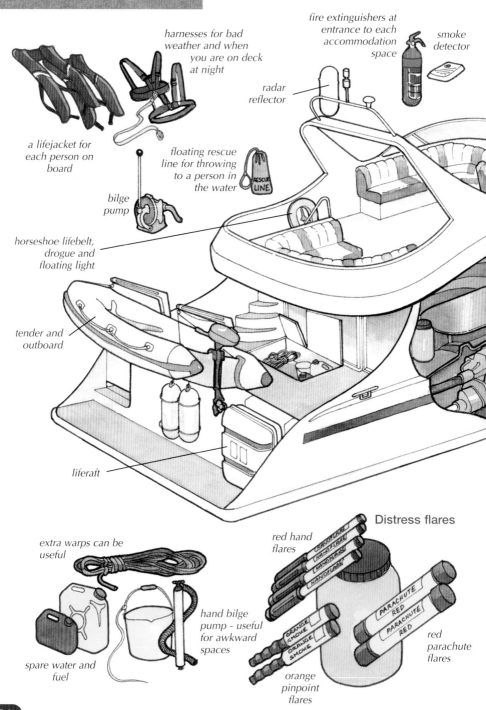

harnesses for bad weather and when you are on deck at night

fire extinguishers at entrance to each accommodation space

smoke detector

radar reflector

a lifejacket for each person on board

floating rescue line for throwing to a person in the water

RESCUE LINE

bilge pump

horseshoe lifebelt, drogue and floating light

tender and outboard

liferaft

Distress flares

extra warps can be useful

red hand flares

HANDFLARE HANDFLARE HANDFLARE HANDFLARE

spare water and fuel

hand bilge pump - useful for awkward spaces

PARACHUTE RED PARACHUTE RED

red parachute flares

ORANGE SMOKE ORANGE SMOKE ORANGE SMOKE

orange pinpoint flares

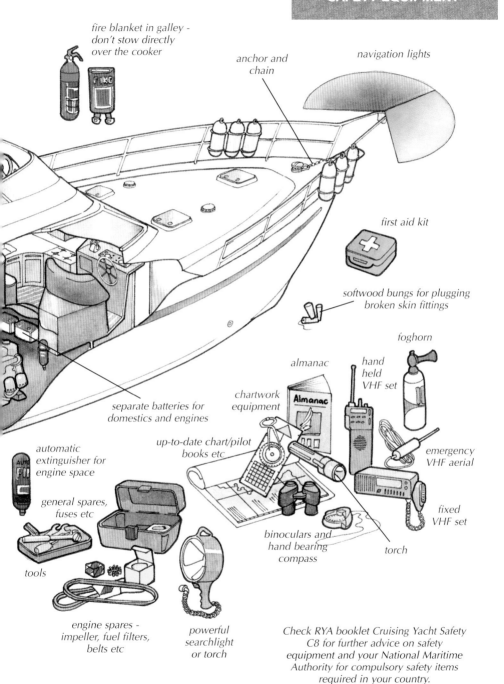

fire blanket in galley - don't stow directly over the cooker

anchor and chain

navigation lights

first aid kit

softwood bungs for plugging broken skin fittings

foghorn

almanac

hand held VHF set

chartwork equipment

Almanac

separate batteries for domestics and engines

up-to-date chart/pilot books etc

emergency VHF aerial

automatic extinguisher for engine space

fixed VHF set

general spares, fuses etc

binoculars and hand bearing compass

torch

tools

engine spares - impeller, fuel filters, belts etc

powerful searchlight or torch

Check RYA booklet Cruising Yacht Safety C8 for further advice on safety equipment and your National Maritime Authority for compulsory safety items required in your country.

Clothing

Man-made fibres layered to trap air for warmth.

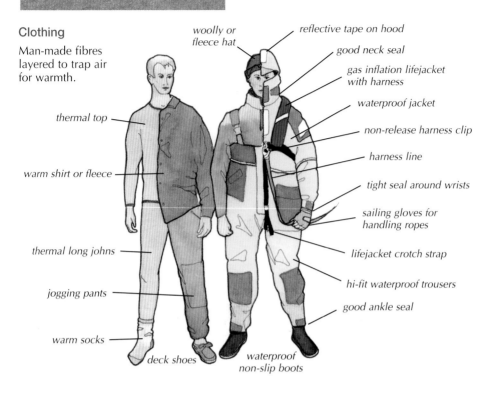

woolly or fleece hat

reflective tape on hood

good neck seal

gas inflation lifejacket with harness

waterproof jacket

non-release harness clip

harness line

tight seal around wrists

sailing gloves for handling ropes

lifejacket crotch strap

hi-fit waterproof trousers

good ankle seal

thermal top

warm shirt or fleece

thermal long johns

jogging pants

warm socks

deck shoes

waterproof non-slip boots

Seasickness & hypothermia

Stay warm & dry.

Eat and drink regularly.

Take seasickness remedies.

Symptoms of seasickness

Lethargic/disinterested - pale colour.

Symptoms of hypothermia

Shivering, pale colour, irrational behaviour, disoriented.

Ultra violet rays are harmful, may cause skin cancer and impair vision.

Reflection from the water increases the effect of the sun.

Wear a wide brimmed hat and/or one with neck protection. Use sun glasses with 100% UV protection.

Regularly apply sun block of SPF 30 – 40.

Wear loose long sleeved shirts and trousers.

Try to avoid exposure between 11am - 3pm – take a long lunch and seek shade. Biminis and cockpit tents are ideal shelters.

Babies and toddlers are especially susceptible to UV damage – keep them out of the sun or well protected.

Wear shoes to protect feet from hot decks and stubbing toes.

Dehydration is caused by vomiting, sweating and simply not drinking enough fluids. It can lead to shock and hyperthermia – heatstroke.

Dehydration Symptoms

Mild - thirst, dry lips, dark urine colour. Remedy: Rehydrate using water and/or with an oral re-hydrating solution.

Moderate – partial heatstroke. Very dry mouth, sunken eyes, skin looses elasticity. Remedy: Rehydrate casualty under close supervision and seek medical guidance.

Severe – heatstroke. All of above plus rapid, weak pulse, rapid breathing, confused, lethargic. Remedy: Get medical help quickly and re-hydrate.

Common causes of fire

Smoking below decks.

Solvents/paints stored below.

Gas build-up in the bilges.

Faulty wiring.

Cooking fats.

Extinguishers

Dry powder – don't use on flammable liquids
C^O2/Halocarbon – good for enclosed spaces
AFFF - foam, good for flammable liquids.

Splashing water from a bucket can be more effective than throwing its entire contents at a fire.

Petrol/Gasoline vapour

Always vent engine space before starting an inboard petrol engine.

Keep outboards on deck to avoid the build-up of petrol vapour below.

Blanket – good for smothering flames and if clothing is on fire.

·ous.

To clear gas - open hatches and turn downwind to vent fresh air through the boat.

Bilge pumps are designed to pump water - many won't clear gas very effectively.

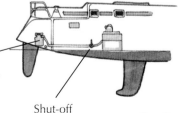

Keep gas bottle in a sealed locker that drains overboard.

Shut-off valve inside near cooker.

Escaping gas is heavier than air and will sink into bilges.

Don't attempt DIY repairs to your system - always call in a qualified fitter.

Location of extinguishers

Automatic for engine space.

Saloon

Forecabin

Extinguishers should be to hand near the exit to each accommodation space.

The engine space should have its own dedicated extinguisher which is automatic or can be activated remotely without having to open the engine compartment and let in oxygen.

Splashing water from a bucket can be more effective than throwing its entire contents at once.

Fighting the fire

Aim the extinguisher at the base of the flames.

Fire blankets can be used to smother a galley fire.

They are also essential for clothing fires.

REMEMBER

The boat will fill up with smoke very quickly.

- Get everyone on deck with a lifejacket.
- You may have to send a Mayday/fire distress flares etc.

If you cannot fight the fire
BE PREPARED TO ABANDON SHIP.

Boating is generally a safe pastime but, should the worst happen, make sure you and your crew know what to do.

Use a pinpoint flare (night) or an orange smoke (day).

Put on a lifejacket.

Alert the coastguard.

ABANDONING TO THE LIFERAFT

Make sure the painter is tied on.

Board raft from the yacht. Stay dry.

Throw raft to leeward and tug painter to inflate.

Put heaviest, strongest crew in first to stabilise the raft and assist others in boarding.

Once aboard:
- cut painter
- paddle away
- stream drogue
- close door
- take seasickness tablets
- keep as warm and
  dry as possible
- ventilate interior every hour.

RESCUE

- The lifeboat coxswain will need to talk to you to assess the situation.
- Make sure there are no lines in the water which could foul the lifeboat's propeller.
  - Any casualties will be taken off.
    - You may be taken in tow but the lifeboat's priority is to save lives not salvage boats.

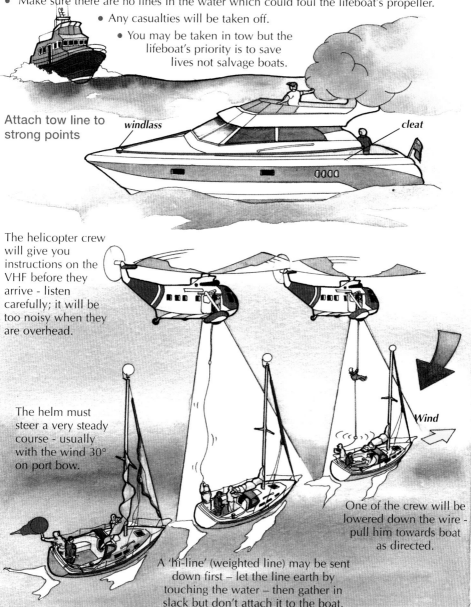

Attach tow line to strong points

windlass

cleat

The helicopter crew will give you instructions on the VHF before they arrive - listen carefully; it will be too noisy when they are overhead.

The helm must steer a very steady course - usually with the wind 30° on port bow.

Wind

One of the crew will be lowered down the wire - pull him towards boat as directed.

A 'hi-line' (weighted line) may be sent down first – let the line earth by touching the water – then gather in slack but don't attach it to the boat.

Methods may vary depending on the country and organisation, some lower rescue cages.

VHF VOICE CALL

Use VHF to alert the coastguard and other vessels in your area.

You must tell them:

- your boat's name
- your position
- how many people are on board
- what assistance you require.

VHF is better than a mobile phone for distress calling - other vessels in your area will hear your call and the coastguard can use VHF transmissions to fix your position.

A mobile phone will only tell one person that you are in trouble; the network coverage is patchy away from land and you won't be able to talk direct to a helicopter or lifeboat.

DIGITAL VHF (DSC) CALL

You may not have time to send a voice call but some modern VHF sets can:

- send a distress alert or urgency call at the press of a button.
- be linked to a GPS to give your position.

090°(T) from Start Point 4.3M

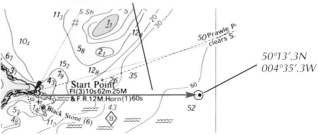

50°13'.3N
004°35'.3W

MAYDAY

When life or vessel are in grave and imminent danger:

Mayday x 3

This is motor yacht *Puffin* x 3

Mayday yacht *Puffin*

(give MMSI if fitted with DSC)

My position is 50°13'.3N 04°35'.3W

We are holed and sinking and require immediate assistance

Six persons on board

Over

PAN PAN

Urgency message - if crew or vessel need assistance:

Pan Pan x 3

All ships x 3

This is yacht *Seaspray* x 3

(give MMSI if fitted with DSC)

My position is 090°(T) from Start Point 4.3 miles

I have a broken rudder and require a tow

Four persons on board

Over

You may use a VHF radio under the supervision of a qualified person or to make a distress call - otherwise you need an operator's certificate. Contact the RYA or your National Maritime Authority for details of courses.

FLARES

NEVER fire a parachute flare if a helicopter is approaching.

Fire rocket vertically.

If windy fire 15° downwind.

Handheld pinpoint flare shows exactly where you are - use inshore or in sight of other vessels.

In low cloud fire at 45°.

wind

NEVER fire into the wind.

Orange smoke for use by day - especially in bright sunlight.

floating orange smoke

for use at night or in dull conditions to pinpoint position

BUOYANT SMOKE

RED HANDFLARE

RED PARACHUTE ROCKET

WHITE PINPOINT

ORANGE HANDSMOKE

wind

long range signal for use offshore

handheld orange smoke

white collision warning flare

Hold at arm's length downwind - don't look directly at the flare.

Other distress signals

Raising and lowering arms.

Fly a ball over a square.

Code flag V is not a distress signal but means 'I require assistance'.

Prolonged blast on foghorn.

SOS by any means.

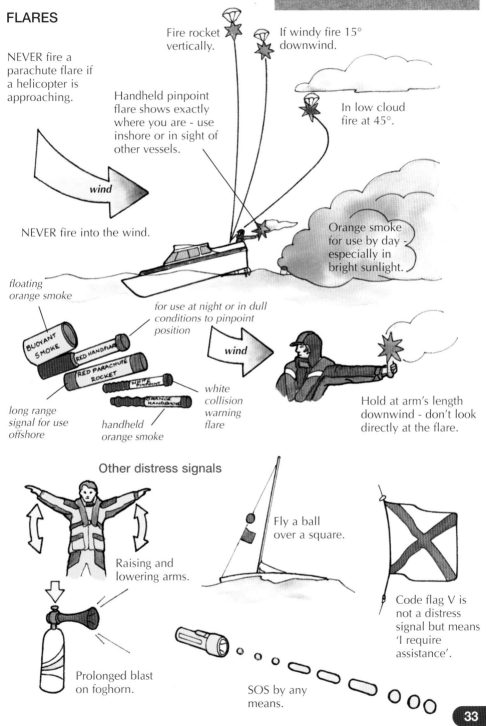

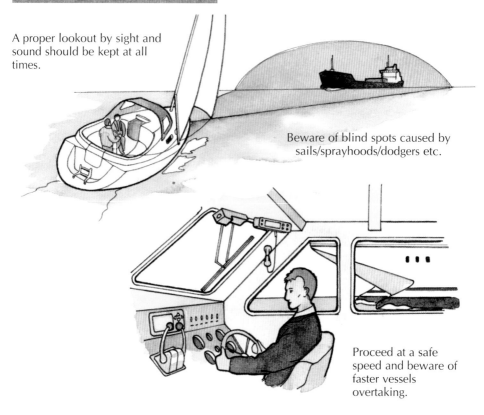

A proper lookout by sight and sound should be kept at all times.

Beware of blind spots caused by sails/sprayhoods/dodgers etc.

Proceed at a safe speed and beware of faster vessels overtaking.

How can we tell if a risk of collision exists?

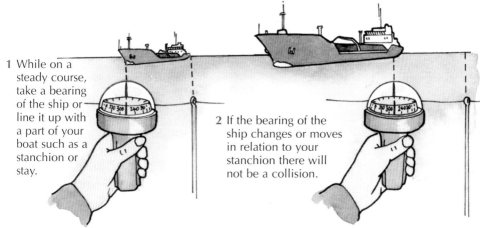

1 While on a steady course, take a bearing of the ship or line it up with a part of your boat such as a stanchion or stay.

2 If the bearing of the ship changes or moves in relation to your stanchion there will not be a collision.

If the bearing stays steady or the ship remains lined up with your stanchion - a risk of collision exists.

Head-on situation -

Both vessels turn to starboard.

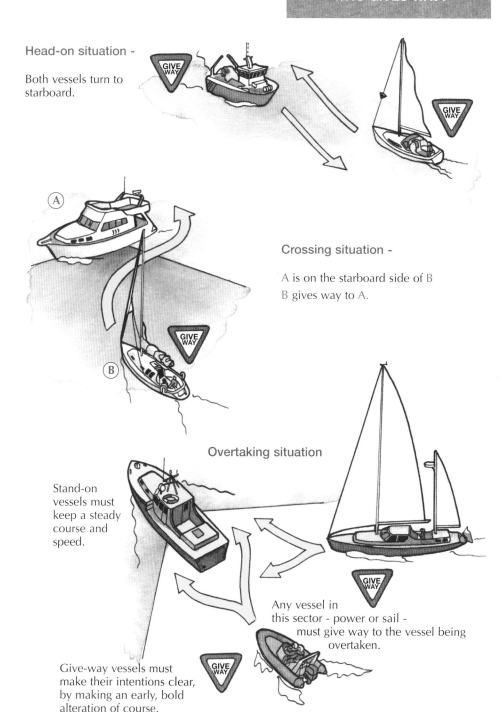

Crossing situation -

A is on the starboard side of B
B gives way to A.

Overtaking situation

Stand-on vessels must keep a steady course and speed.

Any vessel in this sector - power or sail - must give way to the vessel being overtaken.

Give-way vessels must make their intentions clear, by making an early, bold alteration of course.

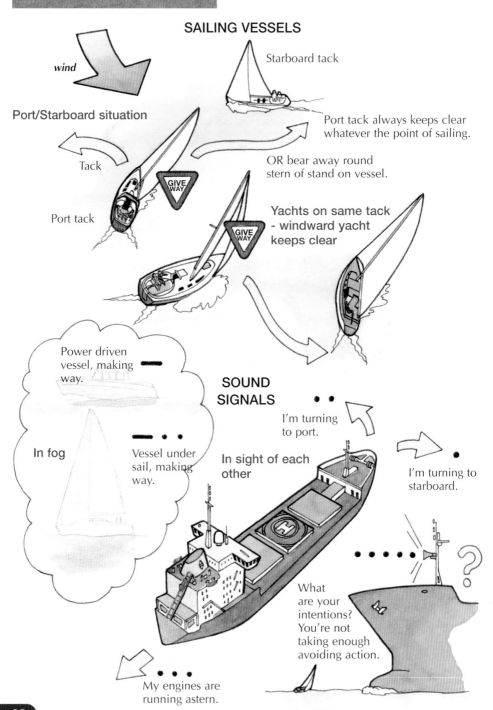

SAILING VESSELS

Starboard tack

wind

Port/Starboard situation

Tack

Port tack

GIVE WAY

GIVE WAY

Port tack always keeps clear whatever the point of sailing.

OR bear away round stern of stand on vessel.

Yachts on same tack - windward yacht keeps clear

Power driven vessel, making way.

SOUND SIGNALS

In fog

Vessel under sail, making way.

In sight of each other

I'm turning to port.

I'm turning to starboard.

What are your intentions? You're not taking enough avoiding action.

My engines are running astern.

NARROW CHANNELS

Power does not necessarily give way to sail when both are navigating in a narrow channel.

Large vessels rely on keeping up their speed to be able to manoeuvre - don't impede them.

If you need to cross a channel your heading should be at 90° to channel.

In most cases small craft can sail outside the main channel – check the chart.

IALA A buoyage

This vessel draws 10m in a 15m channel.

Avoid anchoring in a narrow channel.

5m
10m
15m
20m

If you have to stay in the channel keep to the starboard side and stay out of the way of shipping.

IN ORDER OF PRIORITY

Vessel restricted in ability to manoeuvre (laying marks, dredging etc.)

Vessel constrained by draught

Vessel engaged in fishing

Vessel under sail

Power-driven vessel

GIVE WAY

UNDER SAIL

POWER-DRIVEN VESSELS

less than 20m

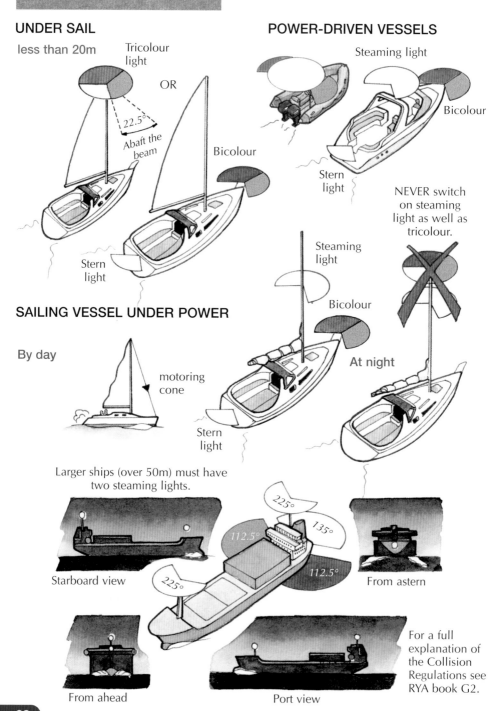

Tricolour light

OR

22.5°

Abaft the beam

Bicolour

Stern light

Steaming light

Bicolour

Stern light

NEVER switch on steaming light as well as tricolour.

SAILING VESSEL UNDER POWER

By day

motoring cone

Steaming light

Bicolour

At night

Stern light

Larger ships (over 50m) must have two steaming lights.

Starboard view

225°

112.5°

135°

112.5°

225°

From astern

From ahead

Port view

For a full explanation of the Collision Regulations see RYA book G2.

At anchor *by day*

by day

Restricted in ability to manoeuvre

eg. dredging cable laying etc *by day*

Carrying out underwater work

eg. large container ships or tankers in a narrow channel

3 all round reds

by day

Constrained by draught

by day

Fishing trawling

Other types of fishing

by day *by day*

white lights have same sector as steaming light

Towing *over 200m* *from astern* *under 200m*

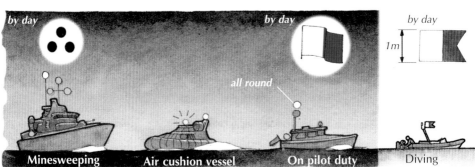

by day

Minesweeping

by day

all round

Air cushion vessel

On pilot duty

by day

1m

Diving

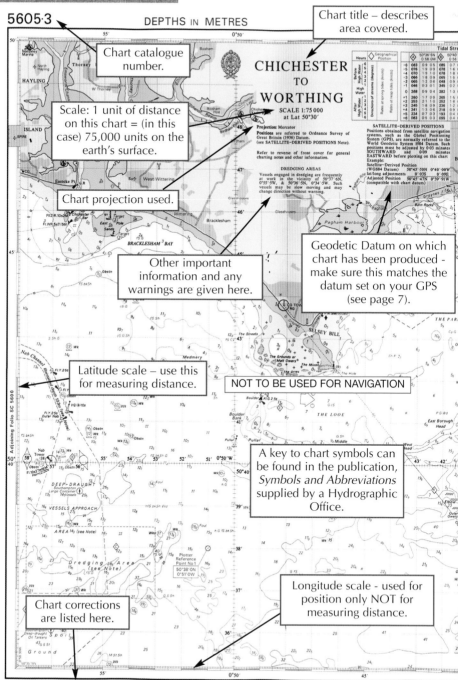

5605·3

DEPTHS IN METRES

Chart title – describes area covered.

Chart catalogue number.

Scale: 1 unit of distance on this chart = (in this case) 75,000 units on the earth's surface.

Chart projection used.

Other important information and any warnings are given here.

Geodetic Datum on which chart has been produced - make sure this matches the datum set on your GPS (see page 7).

Latitude scale – use this for measuring distance.

NOT TO BE USED FOR NAVIGATION

A key to chart symbols can be found in the publication, *Symbols and Abbreviations* supplied by a Hydrographic Office.

Longitude scale - used for position only NOT for measuring distance.

Chart corrections are listed here.

5605·3

This chart is derived from Admiralty charts 1652, corrected to NM2956/99, 1991, corrected to NM1017/99 and 2045, corrected to NM2431/99. Small corrections

Published at Taunton, United Kingdom 6th January 2000 under t
© Crown

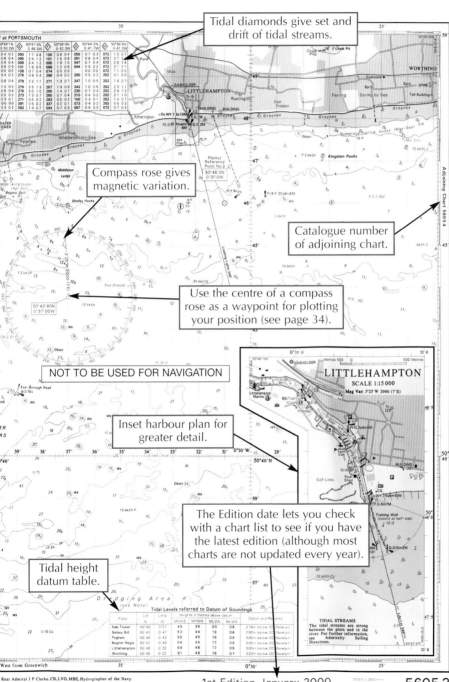

Tidal diamonds give set and drift of tidal streams.

Compass rose gives magnetic variation.

Catalogue number of adjoining chart.

Use the centre of a compass rose as a waypoint for plotting your position (see page 34).

NOT TO BE USED FOR NAVIGATION

Inset harbour plan for greater detail.

The Edition date lets you check with a chart list to see if you have the latest edition (although most charts are not updated every year).

Tidal height datum table.

LITTLEHAMPTON
SCALE 1:15 000
Mag Var: 3°23'W 2000 (7'E)

1st Edition January 2000

5605·3

Rear Admiral J P Clarke, CB, LVO, MBE, Hydrographer of the Navy.
ights reserved.

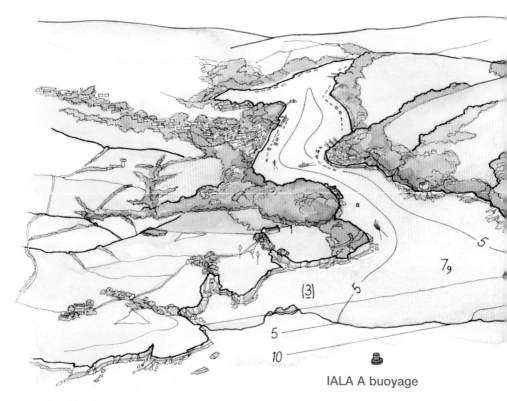

IALA A buoyage

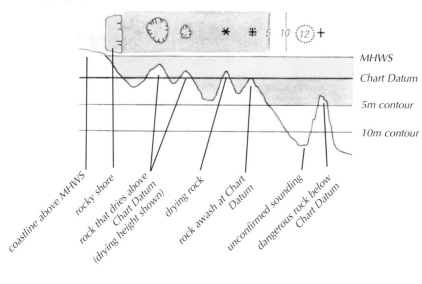

MHWS

Chart Datum

5m contour

10m contour

coastline above MHWS

rocky shore

rock that dries above Chart Datum (drying height shown)

drying rock

rock awash at Chart Datum

unconfirmed sounding

dangerous rock below Chart Datum

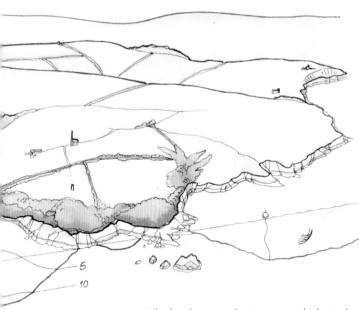

Like land maps, charts use symbols to show useful and important features. Information is carefully chosen to show hazards clearly and to help identify features that are visible from a boat at sea.

Symbols & Abbreviations published by a Hydrographic Office can be used to identify features and symbols on the chart.

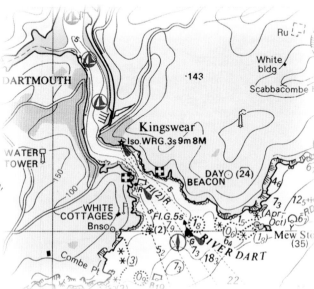

⚓	*Beacon*
⚓	*Yacht harbour/marina*
⬓	*Can buoy, cylindrical buoy*
⊹	*Wreck, depth unknown, not considered dangerous to surface navigation.*
✚	*Battery, small fort*
⌠	*Chimney*
⬛	*Steep coast, cliffs*
◣	*Building*

IALA A buoyage

BY LATITUDE AND LONGITUDE

Lines of longitude run from pole to pole dividing the earth into segments rather like an orange.

Lines of latitude are obtained by projecting angles made from the centre of the earth to points on its surface.

Distance and speed

For all practical purposes a mile at sea is 1852 metres.

$1° = 60'$ minutes of latitude
$1' = 1$ nautical mile

Speed is measured in knots.
A knot is one nautical mile per hour.

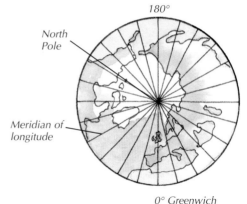

180°

North Pole

Meridian of longitude

0° Greenwich Meridian

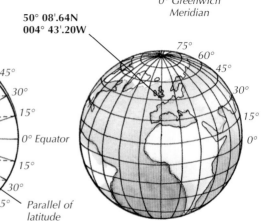

50° 08'.64N
004° 43'.20W

75°
60°
45°
30°
15°
0° Equator
15°
30°
45° — Parallel of latitude
75° 60°

75°
60°
45°
30°
15°
0°

Plotting your position

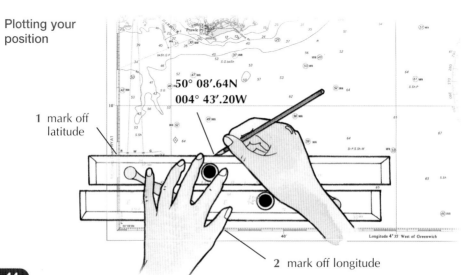

50° 08'.64N
004° 43'.20W

1 mark off latitude

2 mark off longitude

BY DISTANCE AND BEARING

eg. 246°(T) from Skerries Point 1.6M

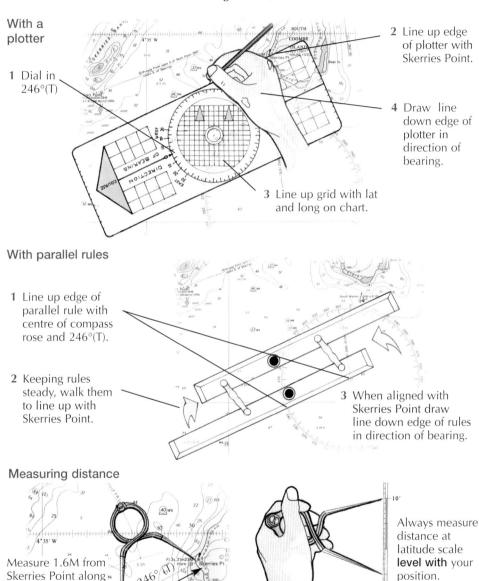

With a plotter

1 Dial in 246°(T)

2 Line up edge of plotter with Skerries Point.

3 Line up grid with lat and long on chart.

4 Draw line down edge of plotter in direction of bearing.

With parallel rules

1 Line up edge of parallel rule with centre of compass rose and 246°(T).

2 Keeping rules steady, walk them to line up with Skerries Point.

3 When aligned with Skerries Point draw line down edge of rules in direction of bearing.

Measuring distance

Measure 1.6M from Skerries Point along line of bearing.

Always measure distance at latitude scale **level with** your position.

Never use longitude scale to measure distance.

Position 246°(T) Skerries Point 1.6M

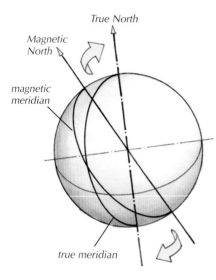

True North

Magnetic North

magnetic meridian

equator

true meridian

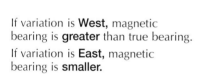

variation | true

Charts show North as True (geographic) North. A compass can only point to Magnetic North, which changes with time and according to your position.

The difference between True and Magnetic North is called *variation.*

Variation for your position is found on the nearest compass rose

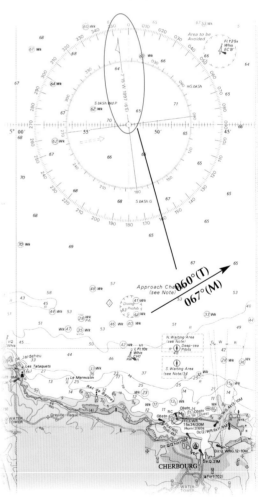

060°(T)
067°(M)

If variation is **West,** magnetic bearing is **greater** than true bearing.

If variation is **East,** magnetic bearing is **smaller.**

for example

With 5°W variation
070°(T) = 075°(M)

With 5°E variation
070°(T) = 065°(M)

Deviation is caused by ferrous metals and electro-magnetic fields on board which will affect the accuracy of the compass.

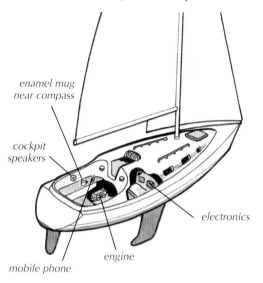

enamel mug near compass

cockpit speakers

electronics

engine

mobile phone

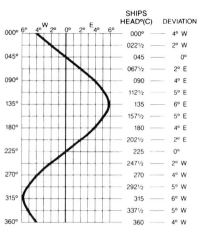

	SHIPS HEAD°(C)	DEVIATION
	000°	4° W
	022½	2° W
	045	0°
	067½	2° E
	090	4° E
	112½	5° E
	135	6° E
	157½	5° E
	180	4° E
	202½	2° E
	225	0°
	247½	2° W
	270	4° W
	292½	5° W
	315	6° W
	337½	5° W
	360	4° W

The ship's compass is swung to check the effect of magnetic influences on board, this will vary as the boat's heading changes.

A card can be produced for your steering compass showing the deviation for each heading.

How to apply variation and deviation

Chartwork is in °True - compass courses must be in °Compass

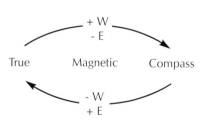

+ W
- E

True   Magnetic   Compass

- W
+ E

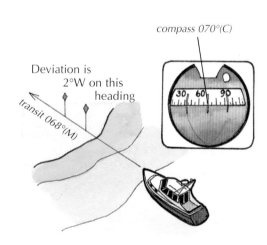

compass 070°(C)

Deviation is 2°W on this heading

transit 068°(M)

Finding a compass course

True bearing from chart	060°(T)
Variation	+ 7°W
Magnetic bearing	= 067°(M)
Apply deviation from card	– 2°E
Compass course	**= 065°(C)**

Checking for deviation

Point the boat straight at a transit and compare results.

TIDES

The gravitational pull of the moon and sun is the main cause of tides.

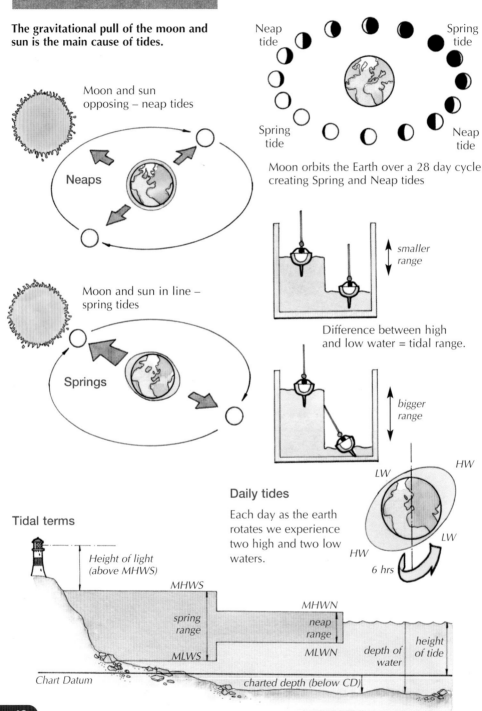

Moon and sun opposing – neap tides

Neaps

Moon and sun in line – spring tides

Springs

Neap tide

Spring tide

Spring tide

Neap tide

Moon orbits the Earth over a 28 day cycle creating Spring and Neap tides

smaller range

Difference between high and low water = tidal range.

bigger range

Daily tides

Each day as the earth rotates we experience two high and two low waters.

LW

HW

HW

LW

6 hrs

Tidal terms

Height of light (above MHWS)

MHWS

spring range

MLWS

MHWN

neap range

MLWN

depth of water

height of tide

Chart Datum

charted depth (below CD)

The depth of water under your boat is measured with an echo sounder – ultrasonic signals are transmitted to and reflected from the seabed to give the depth of water on a digital or analogue display.

The transducer is sited below the waterline - allow for this when reading the display.

You can also calibrate for the display to read from waterline or bottom of keel.

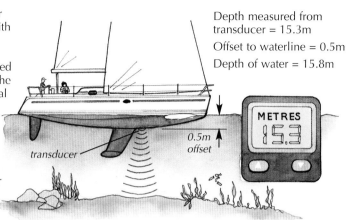

Depth measured from transducer = 15.3m

Offset to waterline = 0.5m

Depth of water = 15.8m

0.5m offset

transducer

METRES

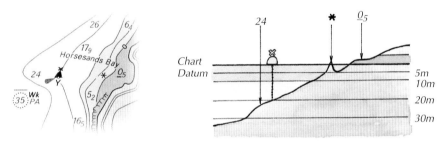

Chart Datum

5m
10m
20m
30m

Chart shows depths you are likely to meet at the lowest predicted tide – Chart Datum (CD).

16	Time	m
	0043	4.5
	0715	2.0
TU	1316	4.6
	1957	1.8

17	0206	4.7
	0835	1.7
W	1440	4.8

Height of tide is measured <u>above</u> CD

Tide tables give the times and heights of high and low water for different ports.

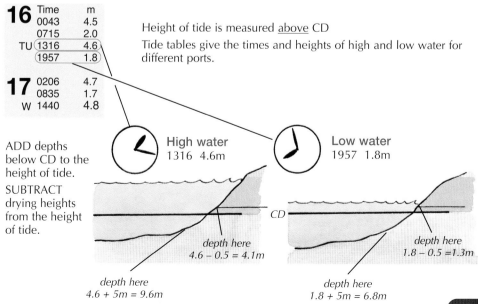

High water
1316 4.6m

Low water
1957 1.8m

ADD depths below CD to the height of tide.

SUBTRACT drying heights from the height of tide.

CD

depth here
4.6 – 0.5 = 4.1m

depth here
1.8 – 0.5 =1.3m

depth here
4.6 + 5m = 9.6m

depth here
1.8 + 5m = 6.8m

Standard ports – tide tables are produced for larger ports and give times and heights of high and low water for every day of the year. Tide times may need correcting for local changes, such as; differences in time zone from Universal Time (UT) and in countries operating Daylight Saving Time in summer time (BST in UK).

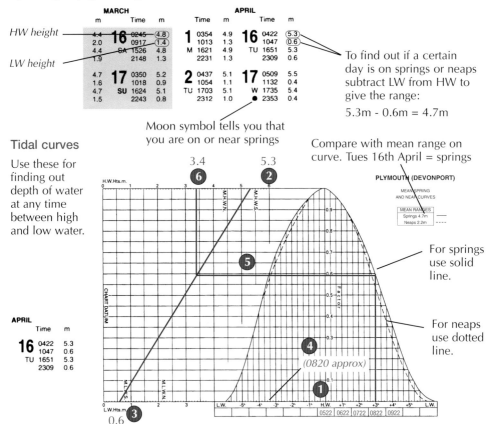

HW height

LW height

MARCH					APRIL		
m	Time	m		Time	m	Time	m
4.4	**16** 0245	(4.8)	**1**	0354	4.9	**16** 0422	(5.3)
2.0	0917	(1.4)		1013	1.3	1047	(0.6)
4.4	SA 1526	4.8	M	1621	4.9	TU 1651	5.3
1.9	2148	1.3		2231	1.3	2309	0.6
4.7	**17** 0350	5.2	**2**	0437	5.1	**17** 0509	5.5
1.6	1018	0.9		1054	1.1	1132	0.4
4.7	SU 1624	5.1	TU	1703	5.1	W 1735	5.4
1.5	2243	0.8		2312	1.0	● 2353	0.4

Moon symbol tells you that you are on or near springs

To find out if a certain day is on springs or neaps subtract LW from HW to give the range:

5.3m - 0.6m = 4.7m

Tidal curves

Use these for finding out depth of water at any time between high and low water.

Compare with mean range on curve. Tues 16th April = springs

For springs use solid line.

For neaps use dotted line.

PLYMOUTH (DEVONPORT)

MEAN SPRING AND NEAP CURVES

MEAN RANGES
Springs 4.7m
Neaps 2.2m

(0820 approx)

3.4

5.3

0.6

APRIL
	Time	m
16	0422	5.3
	1047	0.6
TU	1651	5.3
	2309	0.6

e.g. What will be the height of tide at 0820 on Tues 16th April?

1 enter HW ht (local time) and fill in the boxes for each hour after HW

2 & 3 mark in the heights of HW and LW and draw a line between them

4 find 0820 on bottom scale

5 draw line upwards to hit the curve, across to meet the HW/LW line then up to the HW scale

6 there will be **3.4m at 0820**

You can also find out when there will be a specific depth - ie at what time will there be 3.4m height of tide?

Go down to the HW/LW line from the HW scale, across to the curve and down to the time scale = 0820.

Secondary ports – tide tables are not produced for minor ports. To find the height and times of HW and LW at these secondary ports you will need to apply corrections, usually found in an almanac, to the times and heights of the nearest standard port.

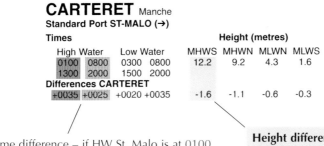

CARTERET Manche
Standard Port ST-MALO (→)

Times				Height (metres)			
High Water		Low Water		MHWS	MHWN	MLWN	MLWS
0100	0800	0300	0800	12.2	9.2	4.3	1.6
1300	2000	1500	2000				
Differences CARTERET							
+0035	+0025	+0020	+0035	-1.6	-1.1	-0.6	-0.3

Time difference – if HW St. Malo is at 0100 or 1300 HW Carteret is 35 minutes later but when HW St. Malo is at 0800 or 2000 HW Carteret is 25 minutes later.

Height difference – when HW at St Malo is 12.2m it is 1.6m less at Carteret. When HW is 9.2m, it is 1.1m less at Carteret.

However if HW and LW times fall between these set times you will need to interpolate between the 'differences' figures -

e.g. if HW St. Malo is at 1630 what time is HW Carteret?

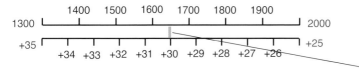

Use the same method to interpolate height differences.

HW Carteret (30 mins later than HW St. Malo) = 1700.

To find the height of tide between HW and LW at a secondary port use a tidal curve in the same way as for a standard port.

Use the related standard port.

For example to find tidal information for Carteret you should use the curve for St. Malo.

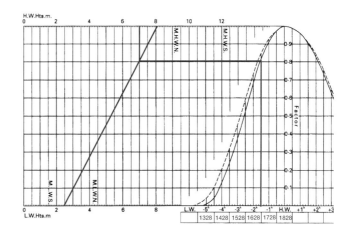

Consider the tide as a travelator

Go against the flow
– travel slowly

Go with the flow
– travel quickly

If you travel across the tide
the boat will be pushed
sideways giving a different
ground track to the course
you are steering.

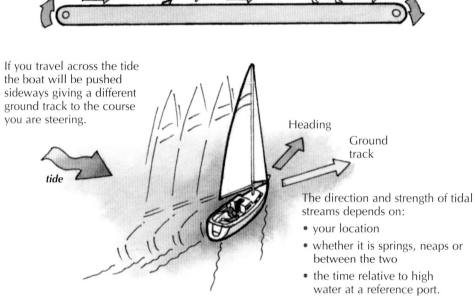

Heading

Ground
track

tide

The direction and strength of tidal
streams depends on:

- your location
- whether it is springs, neaps or
  between the two
- the time relative to high
  water at a reference port.

FINDING THE STRENGTH AND DIRECTION OF THE TIDE

Tidal stream atlas

direction
(measure with
plotter)

03.07

spring rate
07 = 0.7kn

neap rate
03 = 0.3kn

time

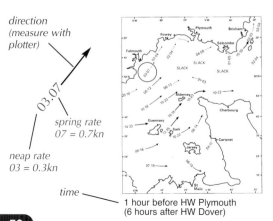

1 hour before HW Plymouth
(6 hours after HW Dover)

Tidal diamond

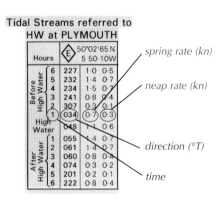

Tidal Streams referred to
HW at PLYMOUTH

		Hours	50°02′65 N E 5 50·10W	spring rate (kn)	neap rate (kn)

	Hours		
Before High Water	6	227	1·0 0·5
	5	232	1·4 0·7
	4	234	1·5 0·7
	3	241	0·8 0·4
	2	307	0·3 0·1
	1	034	0·7 0·3
High Water		048	1·1 0·6
After High Water	1	055	1·4 0·7
	2	061	1·4 0·7
	3	060	0·8 0·4
	4	074	0·3 0·2
	5	201	0·2 0·1
	6	222	0·8 0·4

spring rate (kn)

neap rate (kn)

direction (°T)

time

Example

What is the rate and direction of the tidal stream at a position near Plymouth at 0815 BST on Fri 23rd Aug?

1 Find the time of HW and the heights of HW & LW at Plymouth on Fri 23rd Aug

	Time	m
23	0505	1.9
	1135	4.5
F	1758	2.0

24	0006	4.4
	0649	2.0
SA	1258	4.5

1135 UT
1235 BST is the nearest HW to 0815

2 Is it springs, neaps or in between?

$$\begin{array}{r} 4.5 \\ -\ 1.9 \\ \hline \text{range} \quad 2.6m \end{array}$$

= Neaps (more or less)

3 How many hours before or after HW is 0815?

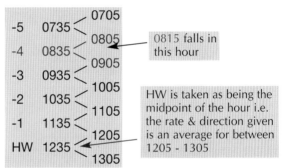

-5	0735	0705
		0805
-4	0835	
		0905
-3	0935	
		1005
-2	1035	
		1105
-1	1135	
		1205
HW	1235	
		1305

0815 falls in this hour

HW is taken as being the midpoint of the hour i.e. the rate & direction given is an average for between 1205 - 1305

4 Find the nearest ◇ to your position = Ⓒ

    Spring rate   = 2.3kn
    Neap rate   = 1.1kn
    Direction of tidal stream = 278°(T)

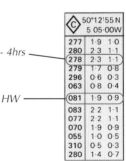

Ⓒ 50°12'.55 N 5 05·00W		
277	1·9	1·0
280	2·3	1·1
278	2·3	1·1
279	1·7	0·8
296	0·6	0·3
063	0·8	0·4
081	1·9	0·9
083	2·2	1·1
077	2·2	1·1
070	1·9	0·9
055	1·0	0·5
310	0·5	0·3
280	1·4	0·7

- 4hrs

HW

5 Or using a tidal stream atlas which is the nearest arrow?

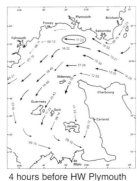

4 hours before HW Plymouth
(3 hours after HW Dover)

Neap rate   = 1.1kn
Measure direction of arrow = 278°(T)

It's possible to reckon your approximate position if you know:

- the course steered
- distance travelled (measured on log).

time	log	course
0900	10.2	070°(T)
1000	15.0	070°(T)

(4.8 miles travelled)

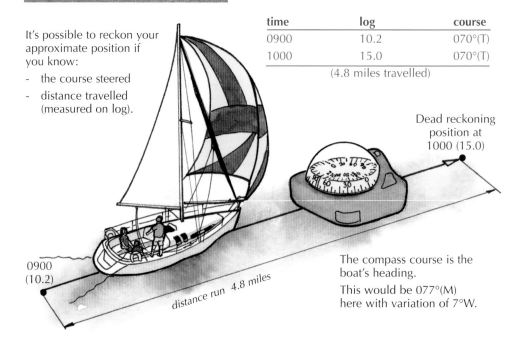

Dead reckoning position at 1000 (15.0)

0900 (10.2)

distance run 4.8 miles

The compass course is the boat's heading.

This would be 077°(M) here with variation of 7°W.

The effect of wind and tide means we don't always travel in the same direction as the compass course steered.

Effect of leeway

Effect of tide

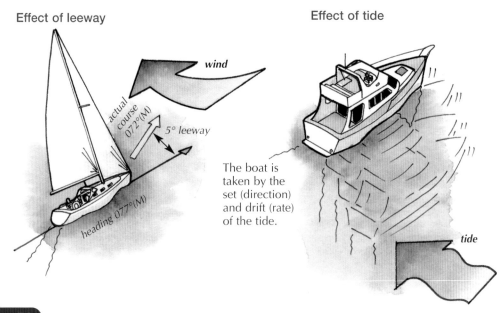

wind

actual course 072°(M)

5° leeway

heading 077°(M)

The boat is taken by the set (direction) and drift (rate) of the tide.

tide

To plot an EP

time	log	course	leeway	wind	tide
0900	10.2	077°(M)	5°	N5	140°(T) 1.4kn
1000	15.0	077°(M)	5°	N5	120°(T) 2.0kn tide for 0900-1000

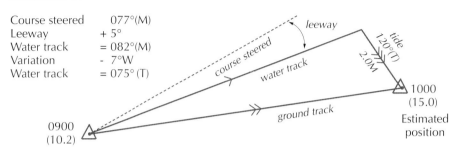

Course steered	077°(M)
Leeway	+ 5°
Water track	= 082°(M)
Variation	- 7°W
Water track	= 075° (T)

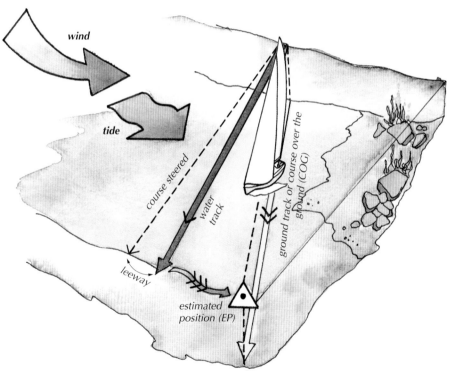

symbols used in chartwork

water track	———→———	EP	△
ground track	———⪢———	fix	⊙
tide set and drift	———⫸———	waypoint	⊞
DR position	———+———		

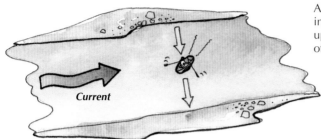

A person rowing across a river instinctively angles the boat upstream to counter the effect of the current.

Current

At sea we often can't see our destination so we need to calculate how much to angle into the tide to make the most direct passage.

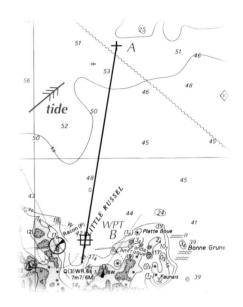

For example:

If I am at position A at 2100 Wed 17th April, what is the course to steer to waypoint B?

1 How far is it from A to B?

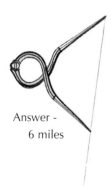

Answer -
6 miles

2 If I think my boat will be capable of 9kn on this passage how long will it take to travel 6 miles?

Answer – roughly an hour because it appears that the tide will push me back.

3 Leaving at 2105 how will the tide affect my passage for the next hour?

Use diamond ⟨K⟩ (RYA Training Chart 1)

Wed 17th April HW Plymouth

		= 1835 BST
HW	1835	springs
	1905	
+1	1935	
	2005	
+2	2035	2100 - 2200
	2105	= HW +3
+3	2135	
	2205	

Answer 033°(T) 2.3kn

4 Plot the tide at the start of ground track.

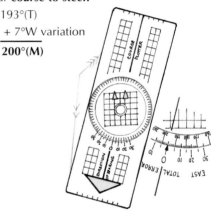

A   033°   2.3kn

5 Measure the expected boat speed for one hour (9kn) and arc dividers from end of tide to cross ground track, this usually goes beyond or falls short of B, don't worry as long as it's fairly close.

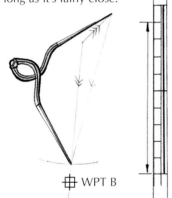

⊕ WPT B

6 Measure bearing of water track - this will be your **course to steer.**

193°(T)

+ 7°W variation

200°(M)

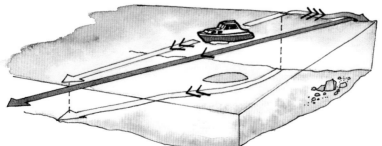

Although you are steering 200°(M) your ground track will be the shortest route from A to B.

Three point fix

Take bearings on charted objects to fix your position.

Draw the bearings on the chart.

Bearings rarely line up as a perfect fix.

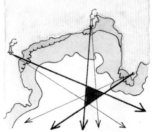

If bearings are too close together - error is greater.

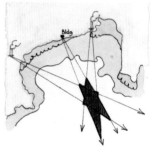

Your position will be where the lines intersect. Use closer objects for greater accuracy.

Error produces a cocked hat.

Don't use objects that will give a poor angle of cut.

Transit and bearing

Line up two charted objects to make a transit - this gives you a very accurate position line. Obtain a fix by taking a bearing on another object, preferably at about 90° to the transit.

chimney and flag staff

The simplest fix

Plot your position as you pass a charted object.

Bearing and contour

Fix your position by taking a bearing on a charted object as you cross a contour – don't forget to allow for the height of tide.

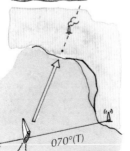

070°(T)

A GPS receiver obtains a fix from signals transmitted by orbiting satellites - this gives a position which is accurate to about 15 metres.

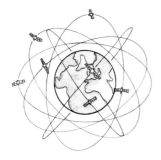

GPS is generally reliable and accurate but, as with all electronics, it can go wrong. The main things that can affect it are:

• power or aerial failure

• transmissions from mobile phones

• interruption or changes to the satellite system.

The simplest way to use GPS is to plot your position from the Latitude and Longitude given on the display.

It can also give:

• your current course and speed over the ground

• information about your position in relation to waypoints (see next page).

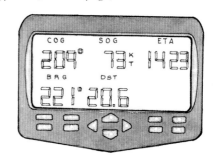

Always back up your GPS position with information from another source such as:

Bearing

IALA B buoyage

A charted object.

Keep a record of your position at regular intervals on the chart and in the ship's log.

Depth allowing for tide.

Waypoints (WPTs) are tools to help you navigate. They are positions stored in the memory of a GPS and used as reference points.

For example you could use a WPT placed at the entrance of a harbour to help guide you safely into port.

You obtain WPTs from:

- the chart – double check you have the correct lat and long.
- publications such as almanacs, directories and magazines.

The GPS display can show the distance and bearing to a WPT and your current course and speed.

Be careful when you input a WPT into a GPS. It's as easy to put in the wrong position as it is to dial a wrong phone number.

When you input a WPT always check that the distance and bearing given by the GPS matches the distance and bearing that you have measured on the chart. Any difference means you have probably input the WPT lat and long incorrectly.

Never input a WPT straight from a book or magazine.

Always plot it on a chart to check your route.

Plot your WPT adjacent to rather than directly on charted objects - you could hit them.

In busy areas bear in mind that lots of boats could be using the same WPT.

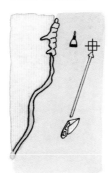

You can plot your position quickly and simply by entering easily found positions as WPTs.
The GPS will give you a distance and bearing to the WPT and you can plot these to give a fix.
This is easier, quicker and less prone to error than plotting by lat and long but double check that you have entered the WPT correctly.

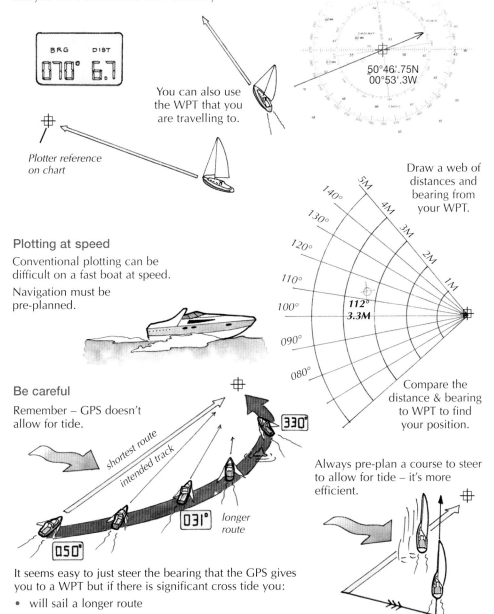

BRG   DIST

070° 6.7

50°46'.75N
00°53'.3W

You can also use
the WPT that you
are travelling to.

Plotter reference
on chart

Draw a web of
distances and
bearing from
your WPT.

Plotting at speed

Conventional plotting can be
difficult on a fast boat at speed.

Navigation must be
pre-planned.

140°
130°
120°
110°
100°
090°
080°

5M 4M 3M 2M 1M

112°
3.3M

Be careful

Remember – GPS doesn't
allow for tide.

shortest route

intended track

330°

031° longer
route

050°

Compare the
distance & bearing
to WPT to find
your position.

Always pre-plan a course to steer
to allow for tide – it's more
efficient.

It seems easy to just steer the bearing that the GPS gives
you to a WPT but if there is significant cross tide you:

• will sail a longer route
• could put the boat in danger.

Two buoyage systems exist in the world, IALA A and IALA B. The difference affects the colour and light characteristics of lateral marks.
IALA A is used in Europe, Africa, Russia, India, Australia and New Zealand.
IALA B, which is illustrated on page 62 ,is used in the USA, South America, the parts of the Caribbean, South East Asia and Canada.

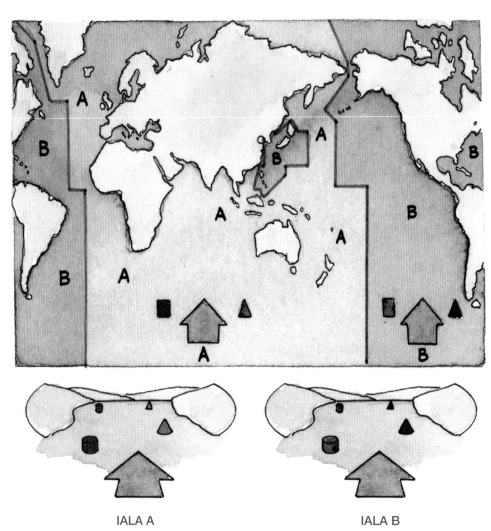

IALA A   IALA B

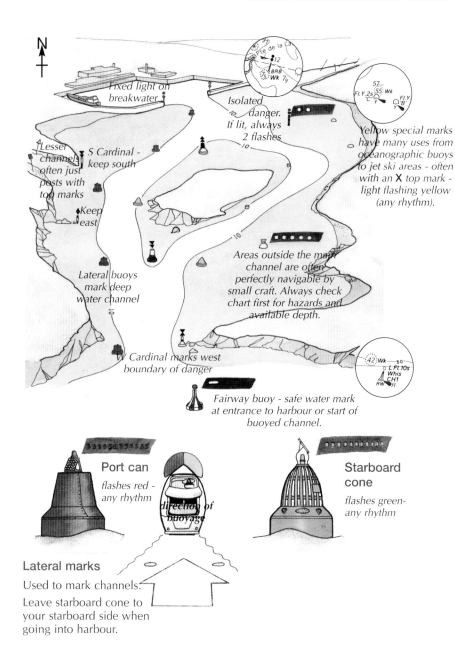

N

Fixed light on breakwater

Isolated danger. If lit, always 2 flashes

Lesser channels often just posts with top marks

S Cardinal - keep south

Keep east

Lateral buoys mark deep water channel

Yellow special marks have many uses from oceanographic buoys to jet ski areas - often with an **X** top mark - light flashing yellow (any rhythm).

Areas outside the main channel are often perfectly navigable by small craft. Always check chart first for hazards and available depth.

W Cardinal marks west boundary of danger

Fairway buoy - safe water mark at entrance to harbour or start of buoyed channel.

Port can

flashes red - any rhythm

direction of buoyage

Starboard cone

flashes green - any rhythm

Lateral marks

Used to mark channels. Leave starboard cone to your starboard side when going into harbour.

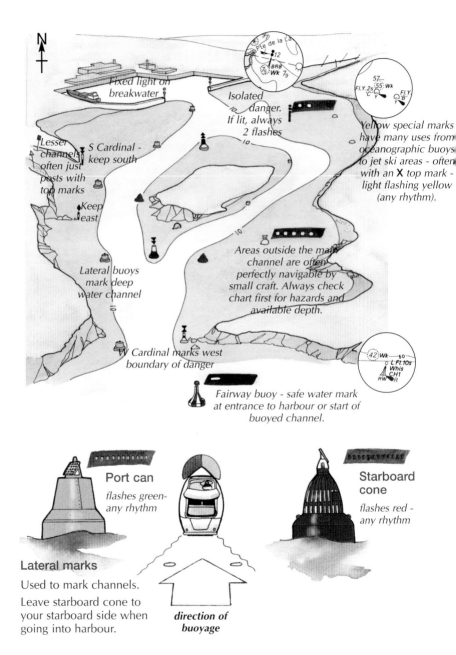

N

Pointe de la La
12
BRB
Wk 7g

57
55 Wk
Fl.Y.2s 'C' Y   Fl.Y 'B' Y

Fixed light on breakwater

Isolated danger. If lit, always 2 flashes

Yellow special marks have many uses from oceanographic buoys to jet ski areas - often with an **X** top mark - light flashing yellow (any rhythm).

Lesser channels often just posts with top marks

S Cardinal - keep south

Keep east

Lateral buoys mark deep water channel

Areas outside the main channel are often perfectly navigable by small craft. Always check chart first for hazards and available depth.

W Cardinal marks west boundary of danger

42 Wk 50
L.Fl.10s
Whis
CH1
RW R

Fairway buoy - safe water mark at entrance to harbour or start of buoyed channel.

Port can
flashes green-any rhythm

Starboard cone
flashes red - any rhythm

direction of buoyage

Lateral marks

Used to mark channels.
Leave starboard cone to your starboard side when going into harbour.

Cardinals

Cardinal marks warn of danger. and remain constant throughout the IALA system.

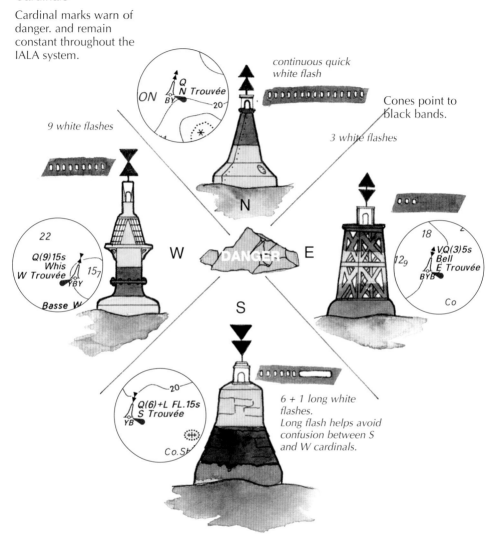

continuous quick white flash

Cones point to black bands.

9 white flashes

3 white flashes

ON — Q
N Trouvée
BY
-20-

22
Q(9)15s
Whis
W Trouvée
YBY
15₇
Basse W

W

DANGER

E

N

S

18
VQ(3)5s
Bell
E Trouvée
BYB
12₉
Co

-20-
Q(6)+L FL.15s
S Trouvée
YB
Co.St

6 + 1 long white flashes.
Long flash helps avoid confusion between S and W cardinals.

Buoys are found in many shapes and sizes.

Solar panels and lights can make top marks difficult to distinguish.

Weed and guano can alter the appearance and colour.

SECTOR LIGHTS

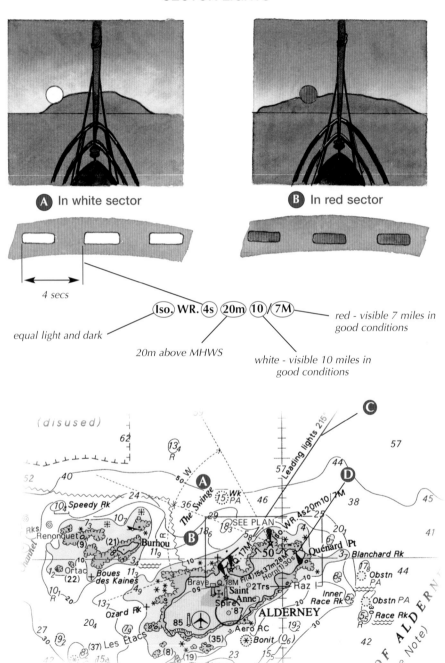

A In white sector

B In red sector

4 secs

(Iso.) WR. (4s) (20m) (10) (7M)

equal light and dark

20m above MHWS

white - visible 10 miles in good conditions

red - visible 7 miles in good conditions

C LEADING LIGHTS guide you in and out of harbour

| Too far to starboard | On course | Too far to port |

Upper light

Q 17M 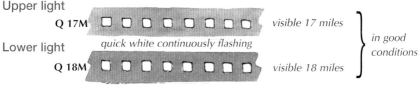 *visible 17 miles*

quick white continuously flashing

Lower light

Q 18M *visible 18 miles*

⎫ *in good* conditions ⎬

D LIGHTHOUSE

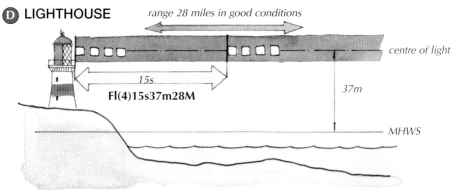

range 28 miles in good conditions

centre of light

15s

Fl(4)15s37m28M

37m

MHWS

Other light
characteristics

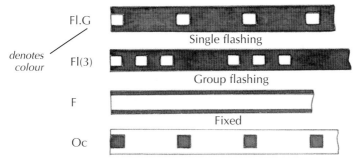

Fl.G

denotes colour

Single flashing

Fl(3)

Group flashing

F

Fixed

Oc

Occulting (more light than dark)

PILOTAGE

Pilotage is the art of inshore navigation when you have visual references to help you find your way along the coast and in and out of harbour.

There may be lots of different hazards so good planning is essential.

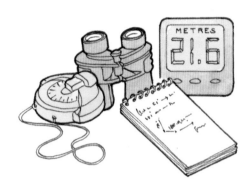

Don't spend too much time down below – you will soon lose track of where you are and put yourself in danger.

Making a good plan means you can navigate from on deck.

THINGS YOU MIGHT NEED TO PLAN FOR

Rocks

Shoals & shallows

Shipping channels

How an expanse of water changes...

at high water   and low water

Chain ferries

Harbour byelaws

SPEED LIMIT
(5)
IN HARBOUR

e.g. Small craft channels

Speed restriction in channel

Effect of tide

A different port may have a change of buoyage system – here it is IALA A buoyage.

Transits

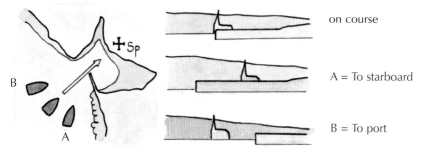

on course

A = To starboard

B = To port

Contours

You can work out where you are when you cross a contour and they can be followed in poor visibility.

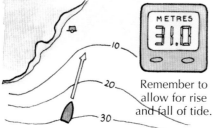

Remember to allow for rise and fall of tide.

Clearing bearing

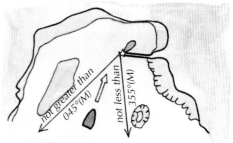

You can go anywhere between the two bearings.

Back bearing

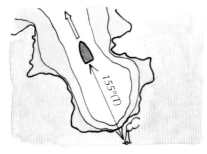

Turning points

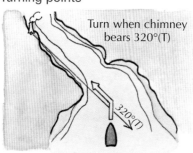

Turn when chimney bears 320°(T)

Bearing + distance

IALA B buoyage

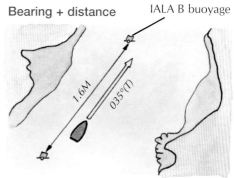

Work this out in advance so you know when and where to expect the next buoy.

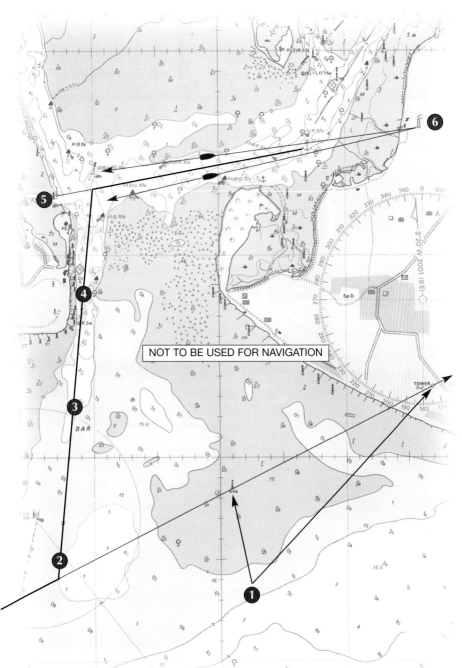

NOT TO BE USED FOR NAVIGATION

Reproduced from Admiralty Small Craft Chart 5600.10 by permission of the controller of Her Majesty's
Stationery Office and the UK Hydrographic Office.

1 Transit

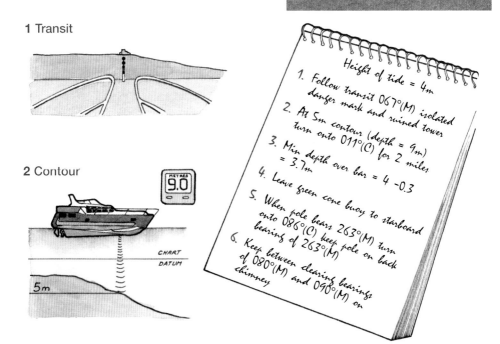

Height of tide = 4m

1. Follow transit 067°(M) isolated danger mark and ruined tower

2. At 5m contour (depth = 9m) turn onto 011°(C) for 2 miles

3. Min depth over bar = 4 -0.3 = 3.7m

4. Leave green cone buoy to starboard

5. When pole bears 263°(M) turn onto 086°(C) keep pole on back bearing of 263°(M)

6. Keep between clearing bearings of 080°(M) and 090°(M) on chimney

2 Contour

CHART DATUM

5m

3 Clearance over bar

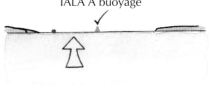

4 Positive identification of marks

IALA A buoyage

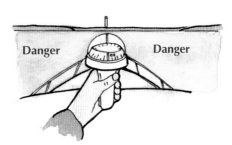

5 Back bearing

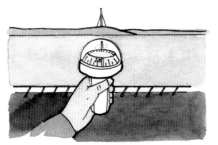

6 Clearing lines

Danger   Danger

General overview

Low and high-pressure systems dictate our weather. They revolve in different directions, depending on which hemisphere they inhabit. Where you are cruising on the earth's surface will dictate whether lows, highs or a mixture of both dictate your weather. In the UK, low-pressure systems dictate our weather. In many places in the Southern hemisphere cold fronts dictate the weather scene.

In the Northern hemisphere low pressure systems revolve anticlockwise and highs revolve clockwise

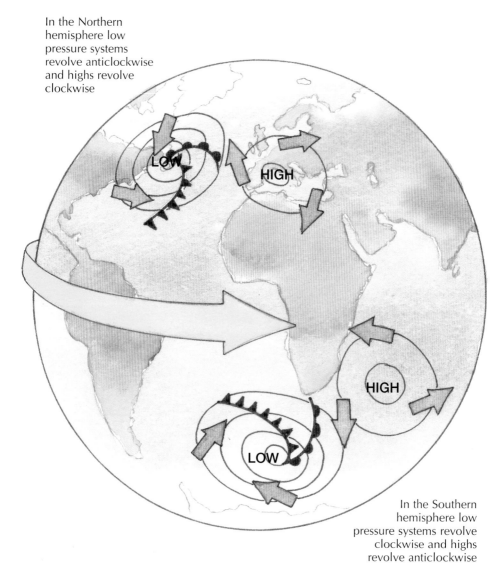

In the Southern hemisphere low pressure systems revolve clockwise and highs revolve anticlockwise

NORTHERN HEMISPHERE

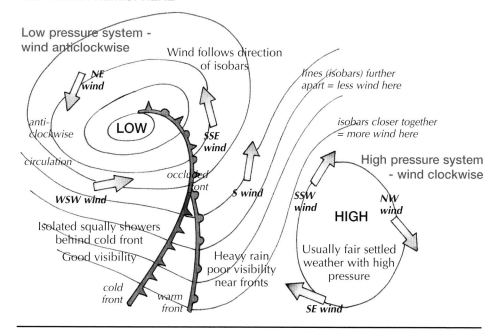

Low pressure system - wind anticlockwise

Wind follows direction of isobars

NE wind

lines (isobars) further apart = less wind here

isobars closer together = more wind here

anti-clockwise

LOW

SSE wind

High pressure system - wind clockwise

circulation

occluded front

S wind

SSW wind

NW wind

HIGH

WSW wind

Isolated squally showers behind cold front

Good visibility

Heavy rain poor visibility near fronts

Usually fair settled weather with high pressure

cold front

warm front

SE wind

SOUTHERN HEMISPHERE

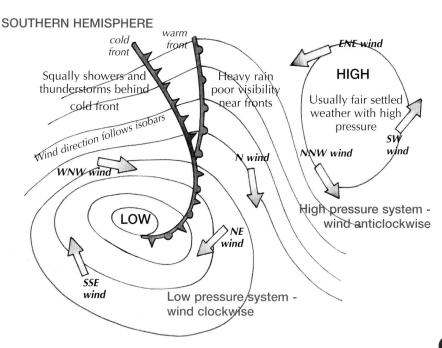

cold front

warm front

ENE wind

Squally showers and thunderstorms behind cold front

Heavy rain poor visibility near fronts

HIGH

Usually fair settled weather with high pressure

Wind direction follows isobars

SW wind

WNW wind

N wind

NNW wind

LOW

High pressure system - wind anticlockwise

NE wind

SSE wind

Low pressure system - wind clockwise

Shipping Forecast Areas Get to know your local Forecast Areas.

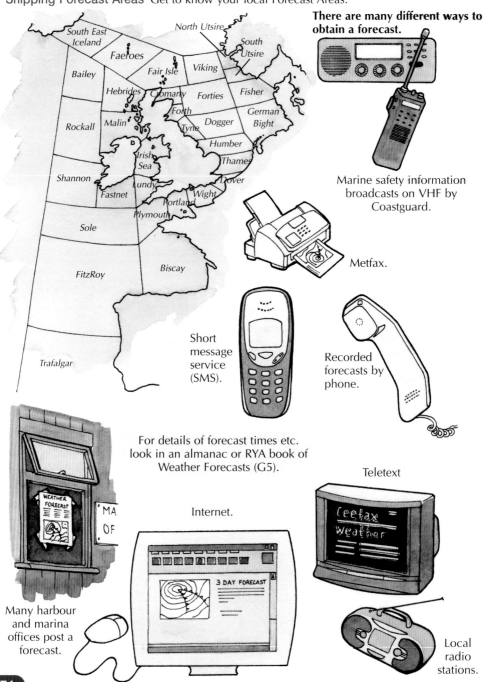

There are many different ways to obtain a forecast.

Marine safety information broadcasts on VHF by Coastguard.

Metfax.

Short message service (SMS).

Recorded forecasts by phone.

For details of forecast times etc. look in an almanac or RYA book of Weather Forecasts (G5).

Teletext

Internet.

Many harbour and marina offices post a forecast.

Local radio stations.

TERMS USED IN FORECASTS

Gale warnings	If average wind is expected to be F8 or more, or gusts 43-51kn.
Strong wind warnings	If average wind is expected to be F6 or F7. F6 is often called a 'yachtsman's gale'.
Imminent	Within 6 hrs of time of issue of warning.
Soon	Within 6-12 hrs of time of issue of warning.
Later	More than 12 hrs from time of issue of warning.
Visibility	*Good* - greater than 5 miles *Moderate* - between 2 - 5 miles. *Poor* - 1,000m to 2 miles. Fog less than 1,000m.
Fair	No significant precipitation.
Backing	Wind changing in an anticlockwise direction eg NW to SW.
Veering	Wind changing in a clockwise direction eg NE to SE.
General synopsis	How and where the weather systems are moving.
Sea states	*Smooth* - wave height 0.2 - 0.5m *Slight* - wave height 0.5 - 1.25m. *Moderate* - wave height 1.25 - 2.5m *Rough* - wave height 2.5 - 4m. *Very rough* - wave height 4 - 6m.

LAND AND SEA BREEZES

Land breeze

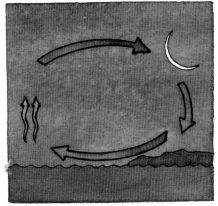

Sea breeze

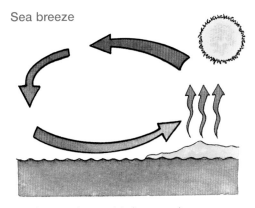

In fair weather and light to moderate offshore wind, a sea breeze is likely to develop. Warm air rises over land, it then cools, descends and blows onshore. Wind up to force 4 in strength.

This occurs on a clear night when the air cools over land and flows downhill and out to sea, particularly from river estuaries.

Wind usually no more than force 2- 3 except near mountains.

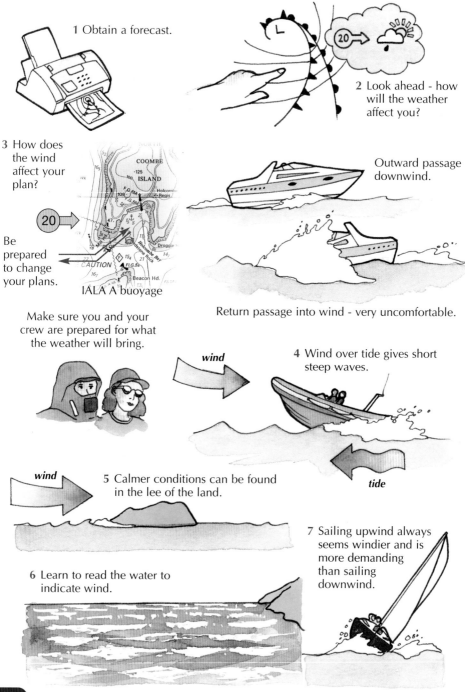

1 Obtain a forecast.

2 Look ahead - how will the weather affect you?

3 How does the wind affect your plan?

Be prepared to change your plans.

IALA A buoyage

COOMBE ISLAND

Outward passage downwind.

Return passage into wind - very uncomfortable.

Make sure you and your crew are prepared for what the weather will bring.

wind

4 Wind over tide gives short steep waves.

wind

5 Calmer conditions can be found in the lee of the land.

tide

6 Learn to read the water to indicate wind.

7 Sailing upwind always seems windier and is more demanding than sailing downwind.

1 **Light airs** 1 - 3 knots
Ripples.
Sail - drifting conditions
Power - fast planing conditions

2 **Light breeze** 4 - 6 knots
Small wavelets.
Sail - full mainsail and large genoa
Power - fast planing conditions

3 **Gentle breeze** 7 - 10 knots
Occasional crests.
Sail - full sail
Power - fast planing conditions

4 **Moderate** 11 - 16 knots
Frequent white horses.
Sail - reduce headsail size
Power - may have to slow down if wind
against tide

5 **Fresh breeze** 17 - 21 knots
Moderate waves, many white crests.
Sail - reef mainsail
Power - reduce speed to prevent slamming
when going upwind

6 **Strong breeze** 22 - 27 knots
Large waves, white foam crests.
Sail - reef main and reduce headsail
Power - displacement speed

7 **Near gale** 28 - 33 knots
Sea heaps up, spray, breaking waves, foam
blows in streaks.
Sail - deep reefed main, small jib
Power - displacement speed

8 **Gale** 34 - 40 knots
Moderately high waves, breaking crests.
Sail - deep reefed main, storm jib
Power - displacement speed, stem waves

9 **Severe gale** 41 - 47 knots
High waves, spray affects visibility.
Sail - trysail and storm jib
Power - displacement speed, stem waves

10 **Storm** 48 - 55 knots
Very high waves, long breaking crests.
Survival conditions

Where do I go from here?

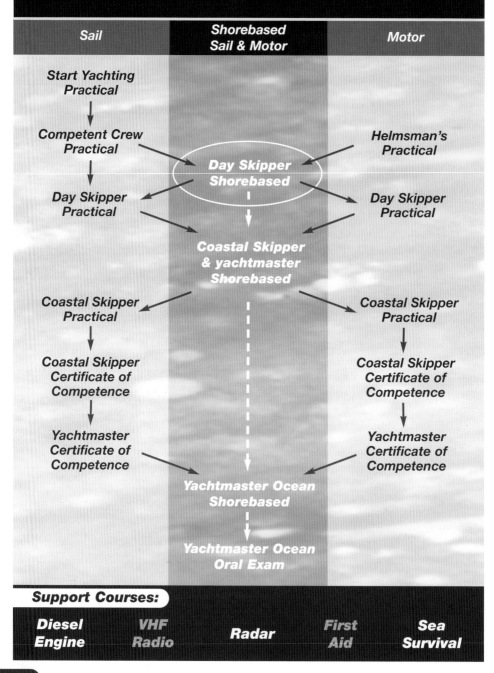

Sail	Shorebased Sail & Motor	Motor

Start Yachting Practical

Competent Crew Practical

Helmsman's Practical

Day Skipper Shorebased

Day Skipper Practical

Day Skipper Practical

Coastal Skipper & yachtmaster Shorebased

Coastal Skipper Practical

Coastal Skipper Practical

Coastal Skipper Certificate of Competence

Coastal Skipper Certificate of Competence

Yachtmaster Certificate of Competence

Yachtmaster Certificate of Competence

Yachtmaster Ocean Shorebased

Yachtmaster Ocean Oral Exam

Support Courses:

Diesel Engine   VHF Radio   Radar   First Aid   Sea Survival

RYA *Membership*

Promoting and Protecting Boating
www.rya.org.uk

Promoting and Protecting Boating

The RYA is the national organisation which represents the interests of everyone who goes boating for pleasure.

The greater the membership, the louder our voice when it comes to protecting members' interests.

Apply for membership today, and support the RYA, to help the RYA support you.

Benefits of Membership

- Access to expert advice on all aspects of boating from legal wrangles to training matters
- Special members' discounts on a range of products and services including boat insurance, books, videos and class certificates
- Free issue of certificates of competence, increasingly asked for by everyone from overseas governments to holiday companies, insurance underwriters to boat hirers

- Access to the wide range of RYA publications, including the quarterly magazine
- Third Party insurance for windsurfing members
- Free Internet access with RYA-Online
- Special discounts on AA membership
- Regular offers in RYA Magazine
- ...and much more

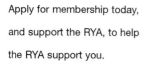

Join now - membership form opposite

Join online at *www.rya.org.uk*

Visit our website for information, advice, members' services and web shop.

1 **Important** To help us comply with Data Protection legislation, please tick *either* Box A or Box B (you must tick Box A to ensure you receive the full benefits of RYA membership). The RYA will not pass your data to third parties.

☐ **A.** I wish to join the RYA and receive future information on member services, benefits (as listed in RYA Magazine and website) and offers.

☐ **B.** I wish to join the RYA but do not wish to receive future information on member services, benefits (as listed in RYA Magazine and website) and offers.

When completed, please send this form to: RYA, RYA House, Ensign Way, Hamble, Southampton, SO31 4YA

2

Title	Forename	Surname	Date of Birth				Male	Female
			D D	M M	/	Y Y		
1.			D D / M M / Y Y					
2.			D D / M M / Y Y					
3.			D D / M M / Y Y					
4.			D D / M M / Y Y					

Address

Town   County   Post Code

Evening Telephone   Daytime Telephone

email

Signature: Date:

3 **Type of membership required:** *(Tick Box)*

☐ **Personal** *annual rate £37 or £34 by Direct Debit*

☐ **Under 21** *annual rate £12 (no reduction for Direct Debit)*

☐ **Family*** *annual rate £56 or £52 by Direct Debit*

4 Please tick ONE box to show your main boating interest.

☐ Yacht Racing   ☐ Yacht Cruising
☐ Dinghy Racing   ☐ Dinghy Cruising
☐ Personal Watercraft   ☐ Inland Waterways
☐ Powerboat Racing   ☐ Windsurfing
☐ Motor Boating   ☐ Sportsboats and RIBs

Please see Direct Debit form overleaf

* Family Membership: 2 adults plus any under 21s all living at the same address

Instructions to your Bank or Building Society to pay by Direct Debit

Please complete this form and return it to:
Royal Yachting Association, RYA House, Ensign Way, Hamble, Southampton, Hampshire SO31 4YA

Originators Identification Number

| 9 | 5 | 5 | 2 | 1 | 3 |

5. RYA Membership Number (For office use only)

To The Manager: Bank/Building Society

Address:

Post Code:

2. Name(s) of account holder(s)

3. Branch Sort Code

| | – | | | – | | |

4. Bank or Building Society account number

Banks and Building Societies may not accept Direct Debit instructions for some types of account

6. Instruction to pay your Bank or Building Society

Please pay Royal Yachting Association Direct Debits from the account detailed in this instruction subject to the safeguards assured by The Direct Debit Guarantee.
I understand that this instruction may remain with the Royal Yachting Association and, if so, details will be passed electronically to my Bank/Building Society.

Signature(s) _____

Date _____

Office use / Centre Stamp

Cash, Cheque, Postal Order enclosed £
Made payable to the Royal Yachting Association

Office use only: Membership Number Allocated

077